VIRGIL EARP

WESTERN PEACE OFFICER

by
Donald Chaput

Affiliated Writers of America/Publishers
Encampment, Wyoming
Printed in the United States of America

Published by

Affiliated Writers of America, Inc.
P.O. Box 343
Encampment, Wyoming 82325
1-800-292-5292

ISBN: 1-879915-09-X

Library of Congress Catalog Card Number: 94- 70541

TABLE OF CONTENTS

iii

TABLE OF DOCUMENTS AND PHOTOGRAPHS

ABOUT THE AUTHOR

Don Chaput is Curator Emeritus of the Natural History Museum in Los Angeles. He has written on all sorts of aspects of frontier history, including mining, the Army in the West, Indian affairs, exploration, and law and order. His works have appeared in such journals as *Western History Quarterly*, *Journal of San Diego History*, *Pacific Historian*, *Journal of Arizona History*, *Southern California Quarterly*, *Missouri Historical Review*, and *Louisiana History*.

He was a contributor to the *Smithsonian Handbook of North American Indians*, a consultant to the *Dictionary of Canadian Biography*, and the mining consultant to the TIME-LIFE publication *Noble Metals*.

Mr. Chaput's long association with the mining history of North America has led him to develop new perspectives on Virgil Earp and his brothers, as the Earp boys followed the gold and silver trail for forty years, as lawmen, miners, gamblers, and saloon operators, from Dakota Territory to Arizona, California, Nevada, Colorado, Idaho, Montana, and Alaska.

FOREWORD

Although Virgil Earp's name is in the title of this work, I never intended this to be simply a biography. I wanted it to be that and more. I want the reader to know a lot about Virgil and the Earp family, and to gain some insights into the history of law enforcement on the Western frontier. And Wyatt appears in these pages when his career paralleled that of Virgil. Tombstone, although not the focus of this book, receives considerable attention because the bloody chapter in that city's past occurred while Virgil was Chief of Police.

Virgil, who died in 1905, was never the subject of a cult or the stuff of legends. Wyatt lived until 1929, and by the time of his death, he was a widely known figure, the subject of countless magazine and newspaper articles, and was also featured in a few books on Western history.

My debts for research help are many. For years, Lee Silva and I have investigated the actual West, and the literary tradition that has grown up around the Earp Brothers, and he intends to have ready soon a major work on Wyatt. My other reliable and dedicated associate has been Carl Chafin. His knowledge of Tombstone and Arizona is unparalleled, and he has shared documents, experiences, and insights on many aspects of frontier history.

In greater Los Angeles I relied heavily upon the resources in the Natural History Museum, especially the manuscripts in the Seaver Center for Western History Research, and upon the rich collection of California newspapers in the Museum Library. The Huntington Library has the extensive collections of Stuart N. Lake, Wyatt Earp's biographer.

The Arizona Historical Society in Tucson has more than a dozen important, relevant collections; some of these are specified in the bibliography. The State Archives in Phoenix has a near complete collection of Yavapai County Court Records, and Prescott's Sharlot Hall Museum contains in its Archives one of the best collections of materials on northern Arizona history, as well as some Yavapai County tax, justice, and business records.

I have also received much information, and cooperative help, from the following libraries, archives, and historical agencies: the Colton, California, Public Library; the Arizona State Library, Phoenix; the Nevada Historical Society, Reno; Central College Library, Pella, Iowa; the State Historical Society of Missouri; the Wyatt Earp Birthplace Museum, Monmouth, Illinois; and the San Bernardino Public Library.

I: EARP ORIGINS

The Earp brothers have been elevated to some sort of national myth, and most of the information and controversy surrounds Wyatt Berry Stapp Earp, one of the middle children in this large frontier family. Virgil Walter Earp, Wyatt's senior by a few years, had as significant a career as a lawman as did Wyatt, yet some unusual historical situations have caused Wyatt to get the press. For example, few people, even historians, are aware that Virgil Earp was the chief law enforcement official in Tombstone, and at the time of the famous shoot-out in that silver city, Wyatt was acting as Virgil's deputy.

The Earp family had a long connection with law and order, and Virgil and Wyatt were in keeping with family traditions as they became peace officers in the Midwest and West.

The first Earp in the New World was Thomas, who was born in Ireland and lived in England until he left for America in the early 1700s. His son John, and John's son Joshua, farmed in Fairfax County, Virginia. William, born to Joshua in 1729, moved to

1

Montgomery County, Maryland, where his son Philip was born in 1755.

Philip served in the American Revolution with a Maryland regiment and shortly thereafter moved to Lincoln County, North Carolina, with his sons Nimrod and Walter.[1]

The Earp family spent many years on the rugged North Carolina frontier, in Lincoln County in the western part of the state. Son Walter took to book learning as well as to farming. Soon Walter was reading law, had married Martha Early prior to 1809, and had become a teacher. He also became a preacher in the Methodist Episcopal Church. The couple raised eight children, of whom six were boys. Walter and Martha Earp meandered towards the West, as did so many in that era. From 1813 to 1827, the couple lived a few years in Tennessee "near the Cumberland River," in Logan County, Kentucky, and in Butler County, Kentucky. Walter farmed, taught school, and preached. In 1827 they set down near Hartford, Ohio County, Kentucky, where they were to stay for twenty years.

Walter's son Nicholas, father of the famous "Earp boys," was born in North Carolina on September 6, 1813, shortly before the family had moved to Kentucky. By this period, Walter was serving as a justice of the peace.[2]

Nicholas Earp married Abigail Storm in 1836, in Ohio County. Son Newton was born on October 7, 1837, and Mariah Ann was born and died in 1839. Nicholas's wife Abigail died in October of that same year. In the following year, on July 30, Nick married Virginia Ann Cooksey, who was to become the mother of the "fighting Earps." Three children were born to the couple during their stay in Hartford: James Cooksey, on June 28, 1841, Virgil Walter on July 18, 1843, and Martha Elizabeth, on September 25, 1845.[3]

In 1845, the extended Earp family, including Walter and

2

Nicholas Earp, father of the "Fighting Earps," held such positions as constable, wagon master, and justice of the peace, in Illinois, Missouri, across the Plains, and in California. Natural History Museum, Los Angeles

Nicholas and their children, moved on to Monmouth, the seat of Warren County, Illinois. According to one account, one of Walter's sons, Lorenzo Dow, had written from Monmouth about the promising country there, and a minor boom in Kentucky land enabled Walter to sell his acres. Monmouth was becoming a center of grain and hog production, had a fledgling academy, and the Earps felt the town was on the brink of activity. The town population was pushing 1,000 when Walter and at least three of his sons, including Nicholas, arrived in this Illinois community, not far from the Mississippi River.

The Walter Earps lived in this small town, and son Nicholas with his growing family lived on a nearby farm, where he practiced as a cooper as well as doing some farming. He may also have operated a rural saloon during this period. Nicholas moved into the town in 1846, where he bought a house and lot near the courthouse. One event of note in Nick's life was his election as captain by a group of 41 sportsmen in Monmouth in 1846, for a "Big Hunt" jaunt into the local woods.[4]

The outbreak of the Mexican War had considerable impact on Nick's career. He was one of the locals most enthusiastic in forming a volunteer unit, under merchant Wyatt Berry Stapp. A company of Monmouth dragoons was formed, under Captain Stapp, with Nicholas Earp as Third Sergeant. The official name of the unit was Captain Stapp's Company of Illinois Mounted Volunteers. Stapp's company saw service in Mexico in the Vera Cruz campaigns, mostly guarding supply trains, although more than a dozen men were killed in action. Nick was invalided out in December of 1847, having received a serious injury by being kicked by a mule. When his next child was born, on March 19, 1848, Nick named him in honor of his company commander, Wyatt Berry Stapp.[5]

In the late 1840s, Monmouth had a local newspaper, the *Atlas*,

4

The Earp family lived in, and Wyatt Earp was born in this Monmouth, Illinois, home in 1848. Wyatt Earp Birthplace Museum

but Nicholas Earp apparently did not make much news. On the other hand, his elderly father Walter, though semi-retired, still served as a justice of the peace. He performed some civil marriage ceremonies, served as a notary public, and was known locally as Judge Earp, one of the dispensers of the law in Monmouth.

The Earps were indeed part of the shifting frontier, and in 1850, the Nicholas Earps moved West again, this time to Pella, Marion County, Iowa, a newly developing farm community due west of Monmouth. Father Walter, though, remained behind in Monmouth.

Nick had received a land grant of 160 acres near Pella for his Mexican War services and decided to start afresh, something almost endemic in Earp males. Pella was a strange frontier settlement, consisting mostly of newly arrived Scotch-Irish from the Atlantic Seaboard states, mixing with over 800 Dutchmen who had come to the promised land for a new life.

Nick stayed in Pella for six years, living on a small farm in Lake Prairie Township. He farmed, opened a harness repair shop, and served as a notary public and justice of the peace. In the census of 1850 Nicholas was listed as a farmer and cooper. Nick owned an 80-acre farm on the outskirts of Pella, three town lots, and three tracts of land in nearby Richland Township, in addition to a two-story home on Franklin Street in Pella.[6]

In 1856 he moved the family back to Monmouth. There is no clear explanation for this return, although it could be related to the death of his father, who had passed on in 1853 and had had some minor holdings in Monmouth. The educational opportunities were also better in Monmouth; English was spoken in the schools [unlike the Dutch influence in Pella], and the Monmouth Academy had a fine reputation. (There is no record of Earps in attendance there, however).

Nick appeared to be settling down. He bought three lots in

Monmouth, and helped to organize the local Fremont Club, which was to become the underpinning for the Republican Party. Nick also served part-time as constable in the Warren County Courthouse; he is listed as such in the *1857 Galesburg-Monmouth Directory*. By this time, because of his brother, Lorenzo Dow Earp, as well as a few other cousins who had moved to Illinois, Monmouth had quite a collection of Earp relatives. Now that Walter was dead, none of the local Earps held any substantial community position, other than Nicholas, a constable; the other Earps were mostly drovers, gardeners, and farmers.[7]

In 1858, once again the call to move came, and Nick packed up the family and moved back to the Pella farm, his second tour in Monmouth being only two years. By this time the family also included Morgan, born in 1851; Warren in 1855; and Virginia Ann, in 1858.

The Earp children had seen quite a bit of moving by this time. In an interview later in life, Virgil claimed that most of his childhood was spent on a farm, and that he had a "common school education." His travels, to this time: born in Kentucky, 1843; moved to Illinois, 1845; moved to Iowa, 1850; moved to Illinois, 1856; moved to Iowa, 1858.[8]

In all of these moves, the family had been in small towns or rural America. When his grandfather died in 1853, Virgil was ten, old enough to get some measure of the man's frontier reputation as a man of the law. Virgil's father, Nicholas, was also an experienced man of rural America, a cooper, a farmer, a war veteran, a notary public, a justice of the peace, and an active local politician.

The Pella education system was centered around Central University. The courses were varied and carried students from the lowest grades into Greek and Latin, moral philosophy, music, and so forth. Virgil Earp spent several years in the Academic Department of Central University in his mid-teens where he picked up solid grounding in language and other basic subjects.

In addition to doing some farming and some book learning, Virgil was doing some frontier sparking, to the dismay and anger of his father. Ellen Rysdam, part of the local Dutch community, and Virgil took a liking to each other. Her parents prohibited such a match, hoping to have her marry a good young Dutch boy. Nicholas Earp preferred that his son Virgil look for a more American type. Anyway, Virgil was too young, only seventeen, to get serious.

The young couple eloped, and were secretly wed in Knoxville, Marion County, on September 21, 1861, using the names Walter Earp and Ellen Donahoo. Secrecy, though, became a problem, as Ellen shortly became pregnant. The birth of the child did not make the Earps and the Rysdams any friendlier. Two weeks after the birth of Nellie Jane in the summer of 1862, Virgil hightailed it over the state line to Monmouth, Illinois, along with a few relatives and friends, and joined the Union Army.

The attitude of Virgil's in-laws can be deduced from this comment in the Portland *Oregonian* of April 22, 1899, following an interview with Virgil:

> His young wife was left with her parents, who
> continually urged her to secure a divorce from her
> husband, and who finally took it upon themselves
> to declare the union at an end.[9]

On July 26, 1862, Virgil Walter Earp enlisted in the 83rd Regiment of Illinois Volunteer Infantry for three years, at Monmouth. He was described by the enlisting officer, Captain Christopher, as age nineteen, 5' 10" tall, with light hair, blue eyes, and light complexion. He was a farmer, and was single; the latter

8

certainly would have made his parents and the Rysdams happy, but bride Ellen may have wondered about his choice of words. Also in the regiment was Francis M. Earp, probably a Monmouth cousin.

Private Earp had enlisted for three years. The 83rd Illinois Volunteer Regiment had a busy, if not spectacular, Civil War career. He served in Company C, and the commanding officer was Captain Lyman B. Cutler. Most of the unit's time was spent in Kentucky and Tennessee, and the regiment was in several major skirmishes, one against the forces of Confederate General Nathan Bedford Forrest near Fort Donelson in 1863. During most of 1864 the regiment was on patrol duty, guarding supply trains, roads, and other communications over a 200-mile corridor. The winter of 1864-65 was spent on provost duty in Nashville.

There are a few specific comments in Private Earp's Civil War papers that indicate some of his activities. For example, during April through June of 1863 he was "manning siege guns & batterys." He also may have learned a valuable lesson about firearms. His pay vouchers for many months through 1864-65 read: "Stoppage for one Remington revolver lost or stolen $20.00." For a few of these months he was docked half pay only, thereby stretching the whole incident over most of his Civil War career. He also had to pay thirty-six cents for a pair of lost spurs in the summer of 1864.

The regiment, including Private Virgil Walter Earp, was mustered out at Nashville on June 24, 1865, and from there the veterans went to Chicago before they dispersed to their various Illinois homes.[10]

What happened to Virgil at this point will be covered later. First, he must be killed in action.

Virgil Earp, a single man, was actually married and the father of Nellie Jane. Ellen's father, probably with the connivance of

9

E | **83** | **Ill.**

Virgil W. Earp

Pvt. , Co. *C* , 83 Reg't Illinois Inf.

Age 19 years.

Appears on **Co. Muster-out Roll,** dated

Nashville, Tenn *June 26* 1865.

Muster-out to date *June 26* 1865.

Last paid to *Oct. 31* 1864

Clothing account :

Last settled ...., 186 84; drawn since $ 100

Due soldier $ 8 100; due U. S. $ 100

Am't for cloth'g in kind or money adv'd $ 100

Due U. S. for arms equipments, &c., $ 100

Bounty paid $ 25 100; due $ 75 100

Remarks : *Stoppage for one Remington revolver lost or stolen $20.00 Stoppage of 1/2 of 1 months pay by sentence Reg. C.M. Gen Post Order No 9 Hd. Qrs. 5 sub Dist. Mid Tenn Apr 15/65*

Book mark :

T. Jones

(861) Copyist.

A document from Virgil Earp's Civil War "Career" indicating that he must pay for a lost Remington revolver. National Archives

10

Nicholas Earp, decided to kill off Virgil. He first told Ellen that Virgil had been seriously wounded in battle. This was partially confirmed, as a local returning veteran also claimed to have seen Virgil at the front, and in bad shape. Ellen's father then did the next best thing and announced that Virgil had died of wounds.

The Rysdams and other Pella Dutchmen had been considering moving West. There was little to keep Ellen's interest in Iowa, now that Virgil was dead, so the sorrowing widow with newborn baby accompanied her family and the other emigrants to Kansas, and by 1864 the group had settled in the Oregon country. In 1867, in Walla Walla, Washington Territory, Ellen Rysdam Earp married Thomas Eaton. Her new husband was not any more Dutch than Virgil, so the elder Rysdam may have had a change of heart about a daughter marrying an American. Or, the number of young men who were interested in marrying war widows with children may have been limited.[11]

In any case, the new bride did not know she was a bigamist. Thirty-five years would pass before Virgil would see Ellen or his daughter Nellie Jane.

The Civil War years were busy for Nicholas Earp. He later claimed to have had a major role in forming three local regiments. He may have exaggerated his role, but he did receive an appointment as deputy U. S. provost marshal for his congressional district, in charge of local recruiting. Also, it is difficult to accuse this veteran of the Mexican War of taking his Civil War duties lightly— sons Newton, Virgil, and James all served more than two years in combat regiments.[12]

In early summer of 1864, wanderlust hit Nicholas Earp again, and he joined with many local families in a plan to settle in California. One of Nick's claims was that in 1851 he had gone to the California gold fields, and on his return had first seen the region around San Bernardino, which had attracted him. There is no evidence for this California trip, but apparently Nick's Pella neighbors and friends believed him. He was appointed wagon master of a train that set out from Pella in the summer.

Among the Earp children making this cross-country jaunt were Wyatt, Morgan, and Warren, as well as Adelia, who had been born in Pella in 1861, and James, who had returned from the wars with a bad shoulder wound in 1864.

The wagon train, consisting of forty wagons and 150 people, left on May 12, 1864, from Council Bluffs, Iowa. The group's moves are well known to us, thanks to Mrs. J. A. Rousseau, who kept a diary of the trip, most of which has been published. Most of the comments about "Mr. Earp" are not complimentary. He was apparently very demanding, insisted on his way of doing things, was gruff, tough, and in general, unpleasant.

Her interpretation may have been correct, the viewpoint of an invalid woman riding in a wagon train. Yet, her criticisms lack sting when the situation is examined. The Rousseaus and others shared food with Indian hangers-on—Earp did not, and he resented the practice. Earp scolded the children when they played and rough-housed, and stated that if parents couldn't control their children, he would spank them himself. He pushed the people, and animals, up the most treacherous mountain passes.[13]

Nick Earp, tough wagon master, may have made the right decisions. The 2,000 mile trip across plains, mountains, and desert, with several Indian attacks, rain storms, and desert heat, ended successfully on December 17, 1864, when the train entered San Bernardino, without having lost a member of the party.

Well, he lost one. Son James, the wounded Civil War veteran, left the wagon train near Austin, Nevada, at that time a booming mining camp. James couldn't do much mining or farming, but he certainly learned how to shuffle cards and serve drinks. His Austin days gave him a feel for public house and gambling hall that remained with him until his death fifty years later.

Virgil's whereabouts from 1866 to 1869 remain a puzzle. In a later interview, he claimed to have arrived in California in 1866, joining his family in San Bernardino. The first known documents that concern Virgil after the Civil War are from 1870, in Missouri. Where had he been for five years?

Probably driving a stagecoach in California-Arizona service.

Stuart Lake's *Wyatt Earp: Frontier Marshal*, presented some glowing prose about how young Wyatt, just going on seventeen, was hired by General Phineas Banning in Los Angeles for driving one of the stages on his San Bernardino-Los Angeles line. Wyatt was tough, big, smart, and had a way with horses. In going through rough country, fending off Indian attacks, and in making record time, young Wyatt Earp was the match for any Western stage driver. Alas, not a word can be found to verify Wyatt as heroic stage driver.[14]

It seems more likely that Virgil was the stage driver. Virgil was taller, bigger, a war veteran, and commanded a lot more attention and respect than his kid brother. Furthermore, in the 1870s Virgil drove stage in Nebraska and Arizona, evidence that he certainly knew the business. Chances are that Wyatt, and/or his biographer Lake, annexed Virgil's career here and made it belong to Wyatt; after all, Virgil was long dead when the Wyatt Earp biography appeared in 1931.

Staging in the Southwest was in an era of expansion in the mid-1860s. There had been a gold rush to the Colorado River, where the towns of La Paz and Ehrenberg came into existence. Prescott, Arizona, was in the middle of several important gold and silver districts. Supplies, personnel, and communications to these posts were from Los Angeles and San Bernardino. The Butterfield Overland Express Company handled most of the southern routes—from Texas through Yuma, San Diego, and up to Los

Angeles. General Phineas Banning from his Wilmington (near Los Angeles) center had major stage lines to the mining camps, as well as a coastal route to San Francisco. His major competitor was Tomlinson & Company, also headquartered in the Wilmington-Los Angeles area.

What most likely happened during this period was that Virgil drove stage for either Banning or Tomlinson, on the Los Angeles-San Bernardino-Prescott route. It may be that Wyatt, youngster that he was, had a job with a stage line, thanks to the influence of elder brother Virgil. For example, the Earp sister, Adelia Earp Edwards [known as "Deelie"], stated the following in an interview:

> When Virgil finished stage driving he and Wyatt went to Prescott, working for a big San Bernardino freight Company with great wagons and long teams of mules and oxen.[15]

Yet, it is curious that not a single mention of the Earp boys has yet been noticed in the hundreds of newspaper articles about California-Arizona stage incidents of the late 1860s. There were all sorts of Indian attacks, equipment breakdowns, duels between passengers, gold rumors, and so forth, when the drivers and other employees were mentioned by name. The Prescott *Arizona Miner*, the Los Angeles *Weekly News*, *Republican*, and *Daily Star*, and the *Wilmington Journal* featured staging news in almost every issue. One can compile names of dozens of stage drivers—John Warren, Capt. Clayt, Tom Mulligan, James Tuttle, etc.—still not a single reference to Virgil or Wyatt Earp.[16]

One new major stage route was opened between Los Angeles and San Bernardino in the summer of 1866, by Banning & Co.; General Banning was hosted at a ball in the Pine Hotel in San

14

Bernardino to celebrate the event. Harness and blacksmith shop owners, as well as other provisioners were certain that San Bernardino was on the way to transportation greatness. By the summer of 1867, Banning had opened a new route to the La Paz gold camp on the Colorado River, with a connection down to Fort Yuma. The new postwar business expansion and the new mining camps in California and Arizona meant rapid expansion of the stage business. Somewhere amongst the many drivers and hands were most likely the brothers Virgil and Wyatt Earp, but not in the positions of leadership given them by overly friendly biographers.

During this period Nicholas Earp, his wife, and children Morgan, Warren, and Adelia, were living on a small farm near San Bernardino, in what is now within the city limits of Redlands. Nick's great call to the new life in California was short-lived. By 1868 he had made up his mind to return to the Midwest, perhaps to sell some land as one source suggests, but more likely because Nick liked to move around. Early in that year Nick packed up his family and headed east, but going north first into the Wyoming country before heading for Illinois.

There is still only the haziest documentation for the where-abouts of Wyatt and Virgil, but it is most likely that they accompanied the Earp family as far as Wyoming. Apparently the family split there. Nick, wife, and younger children took the railroad train back to the Midwest, leaving the wagon and animals with Virgil and Wyatt. Virgil and Wyatt got jobs grading for the Union Pacific Railroad, and handling the teams and wagons for a contractor whom they had known earlier. Brother James may have accompanied the family as far as Wyoming. He could have remained there, or gone on to Montana, a place he visited frequently in the coming years.[17]

Again, it is through Wyatt's biographer that we have some details of these months spent in Wyoming, and whatever is

15

attributed to Wyatt most likely really happened to Virgil. There is no question, though, that both were there, in the rough railroad camps, working hard, gambling, drinking, and according to sister Adelia's memoirs, getting into some bruising fist fights. She was just a child when she passed through the Wyoming country, but over the years she was often present when Virgil and Wyatt would reminisce about the rough-tough Wyoming days. Wyatt was indeed a man now, six feet tall, twenty years old, accompanying his older, tougher brother to the crude timbering and railroading camps of the Rockies.[18]

By the late 1860s, whatever personality characteristics that would eventually comprise Virgil Earp the man had most likely been established. This twenty-five year old Civil War veteran, over six feet tall, an experienced farm hand and well-traveled stage driver would be described in coming years as a smiling, pleasant, rough frontiersman, with a keen sense of humor, afraid of nothing, eager to help, and all-around good company, for campfire, gambling hall, fence mending, and chewing the fat with friends, neighbors, and relatives.

His wife would later have dozens of examples of practical jokes Virgil used to play on her and friends, his twinkling eyes often giving away what was to follow. As a lawman Virgil often persuaded with logic and friendliness; yet, as we shall see, he was not averse to cracking skulls or using firearms if necessary. In gambling halls, as client or owner, Virgil was noticed. There were bound to be laughter, fair play, and a good time for all if he were present. Some of these traits will be seen in the situations that follow, but it is important at this point to indicate the type of person Virgil was, as he and brother Wyatt—as close as brothers can get—had widely differing outlooks on their fellow man. Wyatt was the steely-eyed, unreadable one, unwilling to trust anyone, while his brother Virgil was the grinning, friendly fellow, with

16

apparently not a secret, or a worry in the world.

The wandering family of Nicholas Earp returned to Iowa and perhaps Illinois for a brief time in late 1868, before heading further south, to Barton County, Missouri. There, in the little settlement of Lamar, Barton County, in the southwestern corner of the state, Nick bought some farm property. He settled near his brother from Kentucky, Jonathan D. Earp, who had recently moved into Missouri. It may have been Jonathan who had enticed Nick back from California to try his luck in this rural Missouri agricultural area. Jonathan, in addition to being a farmer, was also a Methodist Episcopal minister, carrying on in the tradition of his father Walter.[19]

Most of the remaining part of Nick's family gradually gravitated to Lamar. Newton bought a farm near his father, and by mid-1869, both Wyatt and Virgil, back from the Wyoming railroad grading work, also settled in Lamar. Morgan's whereabouts is uncertain for this period, and older brother James seems to have remained in Montana for the time being.

Almost as soon as he joined the new community, Nick was given positions of trust. In the summer of 1869 he was appointed the town constable; he resigned that position in November to concentrate on his work as justice of the peace. Meanwhile, he was replaced as Lamar constable by son Wyatt. Although this was Wyatt's first law enforcement position, he was not, as most writers claim, that town's first constable.

The Lamar years for the Nicholas Earp family, off to such a good start, practically came to a screeching halt. Only in the past thirty years, in fact, has evidence surfaced to place the Earps there in 1870-71. Nick, Virgil, and Wyatt disguised their Lamar period, never indicating in interviews, pension applications, or other government papers that they had even heard of Lamar, Barton County, Missouri.

17

The 1870 census, with the Earp entries made on September 3, reported that Nicholas and Virginia were on farm 212, with Warren, age 13; Adelia, age 9; and Virgil, age 26. Both Nick and son Virgil were described as grocers. Farm 213 was that of Newton and Nancy Earp, with daughter Effie, age 3. Farm 214 was that of son Wyatt, with his wife Rilla. Wyatt was described as a farmer.

Those familiar with the careers of Nick, Wyatt, and Virgil Earp will be puzzled at these farmer-grocer designations, and justifiably so. Nick always had to have three or four things going for him. Wyatt had not the slightest interest in physical labor, and Virgil, though he loved the woods and ranches, was not to be a man of the soil.

So, in Lamar, Nicholas Earp did farm, but he also operated a small combination grocery store and restaurant, and also acted as local justice of the peace. Virgil did some farming but also helped out with Nick's business. Wyatt, so some accounts go, did a bit of farming, worked in the restaurant a bit, and walked around town in his role as the only constable.

What happened to dull Lamar in the Earp memories has never been clarified, but it was probably due to a few family squabbles, possibly over marital entanglements.

Wyatt Earp married Rilla [or Willa, or Urilla] Sutherland, daughter of hotel keeper William Sutherland, in Lamar on January 10, 1870, in the Lamar House, the marriage ceremony being performed by Justice of the Peace N. P. Earp. The young couple lived on the farm, and after the autumn election, when Wyatt was re-elected as town constable, they moved into town. Wyatt's wife died, either in late 1870 or early 1871. Cause of death is also unknown, although local lore has it that she died in childbirth. There is also local tradition that Willa's brothers hated Wyatt, held him responsible for her death, and forced him out of town.

On May 30, 1870, Nicholas Earp, justice of the peace, united

18

Alvira "Allie" Earp, as petite as Virgil was grand, was inseparable from him as they wandered the West in search of whatever the Earps hoped to find. Natural History Museum, Los **Angeles**

another couple in marriage, son Virgil Walter Earp with Rosilla Draggoo, a seventeen-year-old who had been born in France. And that is all that is known of Rosilla Draggoo. Whether she died, ran away, was kidnapped, abandoned, entered a convent, or was spirited away by disgruntled family members is not known. Virgil had not done very well in the marriage line. His first wife, with child, had gone to the Oregon country, and now, at the end of 1870, shortly after his marriage, Virgil was again without a spouse. Virgil left Lamar, probably early in 1872, and his trail will not easily be picked up for another three or four years.[20]

Meanwhile, the Nicholas Earp family also did some more moving. Nick and son Newton packed their wagons and headed into Kansas, and in the period 1872-76 were on several different farms in central Kansas, near the towns of Newton, Sterling, and Peace. James Cooksey Earp made an appearance during this period, probably down from Montana, or up from Texas. The boisterous, profitable cattle drives from Texas into the railheads of Wichita would attract card sharps and saloon men like James Cooksey Earp, as well as his brother Wyatt.

Virgil's next ventures are picked up through the memoirs of his third wife, Alvira [Allie] Sullivan Earp. The following account, probably a hacked-up interview with interpretation rather than a memoir, seems to be quite reliable on Allie-Virgil relationships, although the chronology is vague.

Alvira was the daughter of John and Jane Sullivan, immigrants from Ireland who were part of the restless moving masses in middle America in mid-century. The family had lived in Indiana, Missouri, Iowa (where Alvira was born), and Nebraska. The census of 1860 gives her age as nine, suggesting a birth in 1851, although some family sources claim 1849. Her father was a small farmer who cleared land, planted and harvested, and decided to move on and do the same elsewhere. Allie's earliest memories of her father

20

are of "felling trees, burning stumps, and planting grain. . . .I heard Mother say he was a terrible restless man."

John Sullivan may have been saved by the Civil War. He enlisted, and that was the last his family of seven or eight ever saw of him. The story was placed about that he had been killed in action, but it may be that he deserted and started again somewhere, felling trees and making children. In 1862, shortly after he went off to the wars, the mother, Jane, died, leaving a poverty stricken brood to be parceled out to neighbors, friends, or anyone who wanted cheap labor. Allie was passed from family to family until she was sixteen.[21]

Her elder sister, Melissa, had gotten married and moved to town, and Alvira took advantage of Melissa's offer and moved in with the couple for a while. From now on, she was on her own.

The whereabouts and activities of Virgil Walter Earp after he left Lamar, around 1871, are covered interestingly in the following words of Allie. This encounter probably took place in 1873:

> There I was waitin' tables at the Planters House in Council Bluffs when I first saw him. It was early in the evenin' before most customers came in, and I had just sat down with all the other girls and some chambermaids to have our supper first. I don't know why I remember him comin' in the door so plain. He was tall, just over six feet, and had a red mustache. But anyway I asked who he was.
>
> "A Man called Virgil Earp," said one of the girls. "He's drivin' a stage."
>
> Virge saw me too. He always said I was just gettin' ready to take a bite out of a pickle when he first saw me. When I was mean he used to say I was just as sour. But mostly he said I was not much

21

bigger than a pickle but a lot more sweet.

It was funny how I remembered him all the time. I can't say I liked him particularly right off. For one thing, he wasn't the looks of a man I'd figured to fall in love with. I'd always fancied somebody my own size. But Virge was handsome, and he always sat straight on a horse.[22]

The situation, then, around 1873, was that Alvira Sullivan, in her early twenties, after jobs as a waitress in Omaha, and a few other towns, was working in the Planter's House in Council Bluffs when stage driver Virgil Earp walked in, and they caught each other's eye.

The towns of Council Bluffs and Omaha, separated by the Missouri River, were on one of the major stage routes to the West, and Virgil worked the area for a few years. The Council Bluffs population was 10,000, while Omaha was slightly larger with 16,000. Large collections of wagons and migrants to the West congregated there, heading for Montana, Oregon, and California. Virgil drove stage out of Omaha for several years, but details of his route and companies he worked for are not known.

Records, memories, and the threads of history suggest that Virgil and Allie began living together in late 1873 or in 1874. There is no evidence that they were ever married, although they always claimed to be.

It may be that Virgil explained the weird circumstances of his first two marriages, and he wanted to spare Alvira any legal embarrassment if something done earlier ever came to light. This lack of formal marriage didn't mean anything to them, the Earp family, or their friends and neighbors over the years. To all who knew them, they were Virgil and Allie Earp, and they remained so until Virgil's death more than thirty years later.

The wanderlust that hit the Earps so often struck again in 1874 and 1875. Wyatt and James had moved into Wichita, the new center on the cattle trail-rail head. James took to his familiar card playing, running a few girls, and bartending. Wyatt served as part-time policeman in 1874 and was added to the regular force the following year.

Meanwhile, father Nicholas, tired of the steady life in Missouri and Kansas, was again thinking of the West. Son Newton, farming near Hutchinson, Kansas, was in the midst of a grasshopper plague and was willing to talk about a move to the West. Virgil and Allie, who had been interested in moving in with Newton in Kansas, learned of father Nick's Western plans and decided to throw in with him.

The "when" of this is not clear, but it could have been in 1875, or early 1876. There are some references to the Earp boys in Wichita; if fact, Wyatt got kicked off the Wichita police force in 1876 because of a fist fight, caused by his interest in placing his brothers on the force. This could have meant James and Morgan, although Virgil should not be ruled out as a possibility. In later accounts, Virgil sometimes stated that he had been a lawman in Wichita.[23]

The budding wagon train gathered, probably at Newton's place near Hutchinson, Kansas; Virgil and Allie met him there, as did father Nicholas Earp. Eleven wagons formed for the Western trek. One wagon contained Nick and his family; another, Virgil and Allie; and another belonged to Bill Edwards, who was sparking and would marry Nick's daughter Adelia. The wagon master for this eleven-vehicle convoy was, of course, Nicholas Earp, content again to be on the move.

After Wyatt had been dismissed from the Wichita police force, he moved into Dodge City, which was becoming the new center of the cattle traffic, and after a few months in town he was hired as a peace officer.

In early 1876, the Earp-led wagon train pulled into Dodge City, and as the wagons filed down Main Street, Nick Earp yelled out, "Hey you, Wyatt!" He had spotted his son walking with another son, Morgan. There was an instant family reunion, and this was the first time that Allie saw the three—Virgil, Wyatt, and Morgan—together:

> They looked alike as three peas in a pod—the same height, size and mustaches. In Tombstone later men were always mistakin' one for the other.[24]

The wagon train stopped in Dodge for some weeks. Virgil may have been a peace officer there, but no official record has yet surfaced to prove that. For example, Allie claims that one night Wyatt, Morgan, and Virgil brought two men to the wagons for a talk:

> One of them was a handsome young man I liked right away. His name was Bat Masterson. The other one was a sawed-off, sour-faced man named Luke Short. I was pourin' them some coffee when I noticed that both Morg and Virge were wearin' stars. It gave me a shock. Later when I saw them all together in Tombstone I realized this was the first time I had seen them gathered together in what I knew then was the "Earp Gang."[25]

It could have been that for some weeks Virgil was a law officer, acting as a deputy to Wyatt, who was himself, at this time, the second-in-command on the Dodge City force. Chases after train robbers, horse thieves, and involvement in other types of posse work, often led to men getting deputized. Or, perhaps Virgil had been deputized by Bat Masterson for temporary work. By early 1877, Bat, who considered Wyatt his mentor, was serving as an undersheriff in Ford County.

One of the peculiar bits of evidence for that period is a nominal payment to Nicholas P. Earp, from the Ford County Commissioners, on July 5, 1876.[26] Maybe Nick did something related to his typical justice of the peace or notary role, or maybe he, too, had a brief involvement as a law officer—that would not be the first time for either activity for Nick. If for Nick, why not for Virgil?

Normally, the question about Virgil's law duties in Dodge City for a few weeks would not be relevant, but he was to have an interesting peace officer career, and whether or not he wore a badge for short periods of time in Wichita or Dodge City would be good information to have.[27]

According to Allie, the entire wagon contingent of eleven then went to Sterling (or, Peace), Kansas, where Newton had formerly lived. There, Virgil and Allie rented a house for the winter. Adelia and Bill Edwards got married, and the group did their planning for a spring move to the West. On May 8 of 1877, Nicholas Earp corralled animals and people, packed up the wagons, and headed towards California.

They traveled via the Santa Fe Trail, made stops in Santa Fe and Albuquerque, and had a few interesting, but not critical, events along the way. The wagon train, under Nick's prompting, made about fifteen miles a day. The Indians were docile, in fact friendly, and other than making do with a steady diet of buffalo meat, molasses, and bread, the wagon train had no great problems. By July 4, 1877, they had reached the San Francisco Mountains in Arizona and were only two days out of Prescott, Arizona—two months from their starting point in Kansas.[28]

In later years, Virgil had a few light comments about the journey:

> He wanted to go to Colorado from Kansas and
> his wife wanted to go to Arizona, so they decided
> the matter by getting in the back end of the wagon,
> dropping the lines and allowing the horses to take
> their own course. The horses headed for Arizona.[29]

Great copy for the *Arizona Weekly Miner*, but anyone who knew anything about wagon master Nicholas Earp would realize that humor or light-headedness had no role in determining such matters.

FOOTNOTES:

1. There is much contradictory material on Earp family origins. I have followed the "Earp Family Tree" prepared by Effie Earp Cramer, copy in the Wyatt Earp Birthplace Museum, Monmouth, Illinois. For other information on the search for the Earp family origins, see especially the materials gathered by Mrs. Esther L. Irvine, copies in the Colton Public Library, Colton, California.

2. Useful collections of family history notes, including pension file data, are in the Archives, Central College, Pella, Iowa, in the Archives, Sharlot Hall Museum, Prescott, Arizona, and in the Colton Public Library, Colton, California.

3. Earp family Bible entries of births, marriages, and deaths were part of the pension files for Nick, Virgil, and Newton; Archives, Central College, Pella, Iowa. In some documents, Nick's wife is identified as Victoria, rather than as Virginia. However, in his pension file, National Archives, the name is presented as Virginia Ann.

4. Data provided by the Wyatt Earp Birthplace Museum, Monmouth. See also Fred Holladay, "Judge Earp," *Odyssey* [San Bernardino Historical Society], II (Jan., 1980), 1-3.

5. Nick's pension and military files in Old Army Records, National Archives, Washington, D.C.

6. Misc. documents in Archives, Central College, Pella. There are at least 13 notices of Nick Earp in the land transaction volumes in the Recorders office, Marion County.

7. Various records on file in the Wyatt Earp Birthplace Museum, Monmouth.

8. Documents in the Archives, Central College, Pella; in-

27

cluded is the "Central University, Record," of July 3, 1861, which lists Virgil as a student in the Academic Department.

9. In addition to the reliable account in the *Oregonian*, other details are provided in a letter from an Earp relative, George Bertrand, published in full in Alford E. Turner, *The Earps Talk* (College Station, Texas, 1980), pp. 106-108.

10. Records of the Adjutant General, Illinois State Archives,Springfield; these files contain the records of Virgil's unit, his enrollment and mustering out data, and particulars of his service. The information about his lost revolver and spurs is from his military file, National Archives, Washington, D.C.

11. *Oregonian*, April 22, 1899; Turner, *Earps Talk*, pp. 106-108.

12. Records and news clippings, Archives, Central College, Pella.

13. See "Rousseau Diary: Across the Desert to California, from Salt Lake to San Bernardino in 1864," *Quarterly, San Bernardino County Museum Association*, VI (Winter, 1958), 1-17; Holladay, *Odessey*, II (1980), 1-3.

14. Stuart N. Lake, *Wyatt Earp: Frontier Marshal* (New York, 1931), pp. 21-22.

15. A typescript of Adelia's memoirs is in the Colton Public Library, Colton, California.

16. I have read practically every issue of these newspapers.The best run is that of the *Wilmington Journal*; Wilmington, the Los Angeles port city and location of Drum Barracks, was the headquarters for the Banning firm and the *Journal* had transportation items in every issue.

17. Holladay, *Odessey*, II (1980), 1-3, and Adelia's memoirs refer to this trip.

18. Lake, *Wyatt Earp*, pp. 26-27.
19. For the Lamar Earps and their descendants there, see "Hon. John M. Earp," *Lamar Republican*, November, 1905, Historical Edition, p. 46. John, the mayor of Lamar, was the son of Jonathan Earp, Nick's brother.
20. Most references to the Lamar years are contradictory or confusing. I have based my comments mostly on Collection 3551, Manuscripts, State Historical Society of Missouri, Columbia, reels 106 and 107. These are Barton County records from 1868 through 1875 and include dozens of references to Nick and Wyatt, both of whom held official positions. For marriages of Wyatt and Virgil, see Marriage Book A, Barton County, in Archives, State Historical Society of Missouri; see also Marvin Van Gilder, "The Lamar Story," a 1970 typescript, in the State Historical Society Library. A very useful summary of all Earp marriages is Glenn G. Boyer, "Those Marryin' Earp Men," *True West*, March/April, 1976, pp. 14-21, 27.
21. Frank Waters, *The Earp Brothers of Tombstone: The Story of Mrs. Virgil Earp* (New York, 1960), pp. 13-23. A copy of the federal census for 1860, listing the entire Sullivan family, is in the Colton Public Library.
22. Waters, *The Earp Brothers*, pp. 25-26.
23. Virgil's speech in Prescott to the Yavapai County Republican convention, in which he made claim for service in Wichita and Dodge City, is printed in Turner, *Earps Talk*, pp. 80-81.
24. Waters, *Earp Brothers*, p. 34.
25. Ibid., p. 42.
26. William B. Shillinberg, *Wyatt Earp & the "Buntline Special" Myth* (Tucson, 1976), p. 21, note 40.
27. Interview with Virgil W. Earp, Colton, California, most

likely in 1888, in the Bancroft Library, Berkeley, California. Virgil claimed service in both Wichita and Dodge City.

28. Waters, *Earp Brothers*, pp. 55-60, contains Allie's account of the trip.

29. Undated clipping, Archives, Sharlot Hall Museum, Prescott, Arizona.

II: ACCEPTANCE IN PRESCOTT

Virgil and Allie Earp would spend most of 1877-79 in or near Prescott. During some of this three-year period they lived a few miles northeast of town, then west of town, and for some months in the territorial capital itself.

Allie's account of their arrival has forebodings of unemployment, unfriendliness, and overall hard times. Yet, pluck, a few turns of the wheel of fortune, and Virgil and Allie found that Prescott was to be their favorite place in the American West.

Two days out from Prescott, as the Nicholas Earp wagon train hobbled along, they stopped in a little valley with a log house, barn, and corrals. Two fellows there, a Mr. Jackson and his brother-in-law, Ben Baker, did a little ranching, but mainly relied on the mail contract between that region and Prescott for their income. The Earp party visited awhile and were about to move on, when Jackson approached Virgil:

My wife's taken a fancy to the little woman
here, and I reckon I can get along with you first-
rate. I've got a proposition to make to you.[1]

Jackson's wife was with child, wanted company and help, and
Jackson also wanted to have Virgil give him a hand with the mail
route. He offered Allie a dollar a day for cooking and looking after
the children, his wife, and the men, and Virgil would make one
round trip to Prescott a week on a mail run.

The couple figured it was as good a spot as any to start over,
especially since Virgil had less than a dollar to his name. They
emptied their few possessions from the wagon of Bill and Adelia
Edwards, waved goodby to the wagon train, and began their life
in Prescott. The newly-wed Edwards were in a hurry to get to
California, and Nicholas Earp had property near San Bernardino
that he was returning to; Virgil had nothing, so he had nothing to
lose in Arizona Territory.

Allie got along fine with Judy Jackson, and saw to the
successful birth of a baby boy a few months later; Allie claimed that
she had succeeded by reading a doctor's book at the right time:
"Readin' directions, I took him in my arms and gave him a little
slap."

Virgil's routine during these months was to go to Prescott in
a buckboard and sleep overnight at the only ranch house on the
trail. Upon his return, he distributed the mail to other riders, who
made the rounds to nearby ranches and outlying settlements. In
his three to four days off, Virgil did odd jobs around the Jackson
place.

This slow country living came to an end, probably in late
summer of 1877. The Jacksons, with five children now and tired
of the hard land and Apache threat, decided to move back to
Missouri. There were a few squabbles then, which involved Virgil.

Ben Baker became cantankerous over splitting up the mail contract, and tried to get Virgil to side with him, against his brother-in-law Jackson. Virgil remained loyal to Jackson. He also knew how well Allie liked the Jackson family. Maybe it was made easier because Baker was a sinister, plotting type. According to Allie, Virgil ran into Baker later in Prescott, grabbed him by the nose, and called him a "low-life skunk."[2]

The Earps now moved a bit to the west of Prescott, to an abandoned sawmill where his half-brother Newton and wife Jennie were living. They, too, had left the wagon train of Nicholas Earp and had decided to give this part of Arizona a try. The area was hilly, pine-covered, and well watered. Jennie Earp, though, did not take to this kind of rugged living. Allie claimed that Jennie's greatest disappointment was to be living next to a territorial capital that did not even have a church. Within a few weeks of the arrival of Virgil and Allie at the sawmill, Newton and Jennie called it quits and headed back for the civilization—and churches—of Kansas. The so-called lack of churches in Prescott is folklore, not history. There were several churches in Prescott, including the one favored by the Earps. For example, the Prescott *Arizona Enterprise* of August 8, 1877, reported that "The M.E. Church South, was crowded last Sunday evening with listeners to Revd. Campbells discourse."

"Greater Prescott," when the Earps arrived, was a settlement of a few thousand people that was serving as the capital city of the Territory of Arizona. The mining districts of Peck, Tip Top, Humbug, Agua Fria, Bradshaw, Walker, and the Hassayampa were throbbing with activity, and Prescott was the local provisioning center. In addition to this mining business, Prescott was on a major east-west stage route, and considerable political and government business kept this an active community.[3]

Prescott was in a small valley, surrounded by mountains, in an elevated area which gave the region an appearance more like the Midwest or East than other settlements in the Southwest. The buildings were of frame or brick construction, unlike the adobe structures of most other parts of the territory. The San Francisco *Mining & Scientific Press* of November 17, 1877, commented on Prescott in these glowing terms:

> There are fewer idle men in Prescott than in any town on the coast. The demand for labor to develop the newly discovered bonanzas, and the increased forces put to work on the older mines, have taken almost all the floating population.

Virgil Earp found no difficulty fitting into the increased tempo of this territorial capital. In October of 1877, the same year the Earps had arrived in Arizona, Virgil participated in one of Prescott's more memorable shoot-outs.

In mid-October, two strangers arrived in town, hit a few saloons, and drank too much. A local resident, Col. W. H. H. McCall, recognized one of the men named Vaughn [actually, Wilson], during a billiard match in Jackson & Tompkins' Saloon. Wilson and his buddy, John Tallos, named "John Doe" by the coroner, cursed McCall, pushed him around, and threatened him with a pistol. According to McCall, Wilson was guilty of murder in Texas and did not want McCall to spread that word.

McCall had an arrest warrant made out, and Constable Frank Murray went to the saloon to bring in the duo. In front of the saloon, Wilson and Tallos, now outside taking pot shots at a dog, thought that was the offense the constable was investigating. They drew on Constable Murray, held him at bay, mounted their horses, and "started up street at break neck speed shooting to the right and left as they went."

Murray and McCall ran for help and in the center of town found three men in friendly conversation: U. S. Marshal Wm. W. Standefer, Yavapai County Sheriff Ed Bowers, and Virgil Earp. Standefer and McCall grabbed a nearby carriage; Bowers and Murray followed on horseback; and Earp "seems to have gone on foot," and had apparently been quickly deputized by Sheriff Bowers.

Meanwhile, the desperadoes had reached the end of town near the home of Justice A. O. Noyes, dismounted, and while hefting pistols in their hands, did not know who the two men were who were approaching so fast in the carriage. They yelled at Marshal Standefer, "don't run over us you s____ of a b_____." Standefer and McCall went on a few more yards, stopped, got out, and approached the duo. At the same time, Sheriff Bowers and Constable Murray rode up from town. The law, from both sides, yelled at the men to surrender.

Cornered and desperate, Wilson and Tallos began shooting in two directions, and there followed a general shootout, with McCall and Standefer on one side, Bowers and Murray on the other, and the two trouble-makers in the middle:

> In the meantime Earp, who appears to have
> been playing a lone hand with a Winchester rifle
> was doing good service between the two fires.

When the carnage was over, Tallos lay dead by a fence, with eight bullet and buckshot wounds, and Wilson was fading fast, with a hole in his head, a cigarette still between his lips. These and many additional details were gathered by a coroner's jury, and the results were published in the *Arizona Weekly Miner* of October 19, 1877.

Wilson died a few days later, and the following week the dead men's horses, saddles, and outfits were sold at public auction for $75. As one of the oddities of frontier life, it was later learned that Wilson had spent some time in Wichita. In 1875, Policeman Wyatt Earp of the Wichita force had collected a wagon sale debt from Wilson. Now, the hastily deputized Virgil Earp had ended Wilson's brief badman career. Wilson had also chalked up a series of misdeeds in Colorado; among the many charges against him was the murder of the sheriff and deputy of Las Animas County.[4]

The above incident was to have enormous impact on the Western peace officer career of Virgil Earp. His hobnobbing with marshals, sheriffs, and constables was keeping him in good company, but his marksmanship on that occasion would be remembered in Prescott and elsewhere for years.

Virgil's reputation made him a candidate for one of the frontier's tough jobs, that of a stage driver. He had earlier worked out of Prescott and San Bernardino in the 1860s, and he was driving stage in Nebraska and Iowa when he met and married Allie in 1873-74. Stage drivers were often large men, with reputations to match. So, this Civil War veteran, an experienced stage driver, and a man already somewhat familiar with the territory, was a likely prospect when a new opportunity arose. The fact that he had wielded his Winchester with such efficiency against some desperadoes did not hurt his chances.

In late winter-early spring of 1878, the miners around Tip Top and Gillett experienced a new optimism. More men were employed than in the previous year, new stores were opened in Gillett, and the mining district in general was in bonanza. The traffic was such that the *Arizona Weekly Miner* of March 8, 1878, had this to report:

> The road between Prescott and Gillett is rep-
> resented to be lined with teams, and people. The

36

Newspaper office in Prescott, Arizona. Sharlot Hall Museum

route is more generally used by the traveling public than any in the Territory.

The same issue announced formation of a new transportation company—Patterson, Caldwell, & Levally—which became known as the P. C. & Co. line. This had been a buckboard line, but the P. C. & Co. at once bought a stage, and intended to buy more vehicles within a few months. Their objective was "to run four-horse teams from here to Tiptop and back, three times a week," and that would require twenty horses and two drivers.

A week later the *Miner* announced that the P. C. & Co. had bought out a struggling Phoenix stage line. From now on, P. C. & Co. would provide runs, twice a week, from Prescott to Phoenix, Agua Fria, Big Bug, Cottonwoods, Black Canyon, Gillett, Tip Top, and Humbug. Within another few weeks, the P. C. & Co. was handling the U. S. mails, on a run from Prescott to Tip Top to Phoenix.

The first driver that the P. C. & Co. hired was probably Virgil Earp. He became good copy for the *Miner*, and upon his arrival in Prescott at the end of his runs, someone from the newspaper would ask Virgil about road conditions, the weather, Indian problems, troop movements, mining production, and so forth. For example, in the issue of March 29, Virgil was quoted on the type of mining machinery installed at the mill in Gillett, and on the number of silver and gold bullion bars turned out so far. In the issue of April 5, Virgil was quoted three times, on the amount of ore at the Gillett mill, on the winner of a $200 horse race at Bumblebee, and on the names of passengers from his Phoenix-Gillett run.

Virgil was an extrovert, and because of his size, good looks, and friendly but gruff style, he became a well-known personality on the stage line. He also met and became very friendly with some notable territorial power brokers. For example, on one short trip his passengers were the Hon. J. J. Gosper and C. W. Beach. Gosper was Territorial Secretary of Arizona, and Beach was the publisher of the *Miner*.

In April, with Virgil driving the stage, Beach, Gosper, and D. B. Gillett made a several-day tour of the mines in the Humbug District, then visited almost a hundred diggings, mills, shafts, and

STAGE LINE
AND EXPRESS
LEAVES PLAZA STABLE
Every Monday and Thursday Morning,
—FOR—
GILLETT, TIP-TOP AND PHŒNIX.
P. C. & CO.

PATTERSON, CALDWELL & LEVALLY have established a well appointed line of coaches between Prescott, Gillett, Tip-top and Phœnix, carrying

Passengers, Packages, Light Freight, Letters, Papers, Bullion, Etc.

We intend to make this a permanent business, and to that end are stocking the road with the very best stage horses to be found in the country.

Virgil Earp was one of the most popular stage drivers when he worked for this outfit in 1878. Prescott Enterprise, April 24, 1878

other mining operations between Humbug, Tip Top, and Gillett. Beach later wrote a lengthy column on the trip for the *Miner*.[5]

The summer of 1878 saw the arrival of another personality

that was to figure so prominently in the career of the Earp brothers, Crawley P. Dake. He had been appointed the U. S. marshal for the Territory of Arizona to succeed Marshal Standefer and was to become a lifelong supporter of the Earps.

It is not known how long Virgil kept his position with the stage company, but it was probably not into late summer. As with many activities related to mining and milling, the busts go with the booms. There had been a slacking of activity at Tip Top and Gillett in the summer, traffic fell off a bit, and Virgil and other employees may have started to look elsewhere for something more secure. What is known for certain is that in early October, the P. C. & Co. collapsed, and the owners "skipped the country," heading into New Mexico with wagons, horses, and other equipment. They left debts and bad feelings in Prescott. Virgil did not figure in any of the many news accounts, so he had most likely left the firm before the financial disaster.[6]

Virgil's spring and summer as a stage driver had given him an intimacy with Gosper and Dake, and that fact needs highlighting. The new territorial governor, who would last through the Tombstone troubles in late 1881, was General John C. Fremont, the Pathfinder, or the Pathloser, depending on one's point of view. Fremont's heart was everywhere but in Arizona Territory, and he spent little time there, planning schemes for California, New England, Mexico—anywhere but his area of concern. His period as governor was characterized by his absence, or disinterest in territorial matters.[7]

As a result, the second tier of territorial officials became the strong men in the political and financial arena. Gosper, the territorial secretary, and Dake, the U. S. marshal, were the decision makers. They got their way in most matters. Both men were also taking care of business—their own—as they amassed small fortunes. Gosper and Dake owned mines, mills, mining

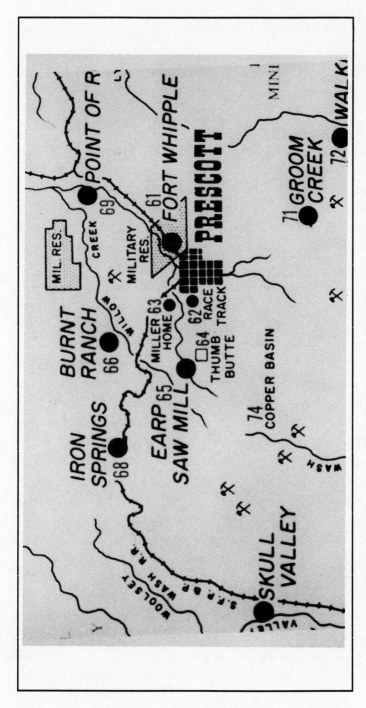

This map of historic sites near Prescott implies that the Virgil Earp saw mill enterprise was greater than it was. In the late 1870s, Virgil sawed some wood, raised a few animals, kept a hired hand, but mostly drove a stage. Arizoniana, Winter, 1963

41

claims, race horses, homes, and apartments in Prescott and ranches in the country, and became familiar with all the ways of making a dollar on the Arizona frontier.[8]

They knew of Virgil's reputation as a man without fear, and on their many stage trips they became more familiar with this pleasant, intelligent, responsible driver. Secretary Gosper and Marshal Dake would become Virgil Earp's patrons, based on their acquaintance made on rough trips on the Tip Top-Prescott stage run. The relationships that evolved will become more noticeable later, but one point can indicate how significant these friendships were. In late 1879, when Doc Holliday stopped in Prescott, prior to going on to Tombstone, he roomed at the same house as Secretary Gosper.[9] So Wyatt's buddy Doc became closely linked with Gosper, who was very familiar with that other Earp, stage driver Virgil.

How Virgil put food on the table all the time is not known, although in Prescott he did from time to time harvest pine from his claim to the west of town. His small sawmill was at the base of Thumb Butte, the most distinctive landmark near Prescott. Some lumber he sold to Prescott builders. In 1878-79, Virgil supplied the lumber for the finest home in Prescott, that of the Hon. Edmund Wells, associate justice of the Territorial Supreme Court. At other times Virgil's market was the U. S. Army, which had troops stationed at Whipple Barracks near Prescott. The biggest need for lumber, though, was for the dozens of active mining camps in the Prescott environs.

Virgil considered a law enforcement position in early 1878, right before he joined the new P. C. & Co. as a stage driver. He applied to be nightwatchman, but the village council was cutting costs and eliminated one of the two nightwatchman positions. On September 3, the village nightwatchman, W. W. Vanderbilt, resigned, and the common council appointed Virgil Earp as his replacement. This was Earp's first paid employment in Arizona Territory as a law enforcement officer. His salary was fixed at $75 a month.[10]

Virgil believed he could serve in two similar capacities at the same time, so in November he entered his name as candidate for the position of constable in the Precinct of Prescott. In the election, the final tally was Earp, 386; Murray, 271; Pierce, 263. The two top vote-getters were elected, so Virgil Earp and Frank Murray were declared the winners; Murray had also been a participant in the Prescott shootout the year before.[11]

The *Miner* of December 6, 1878, reported that Virgil had resigned as nightwatchman. He may have had too long a day, being both precinct constable and village nightwatchman. Earp decided to continue only with the constable job.

The positions of nightwatchman and constable were, in the late nineteenth century, the bottom rung of law enforcement positions in most communities and settlements. But, one seldom started at the top in any occupation. In Prescott, Virgil Earp was part of an effective law and order system. The top lawman in the Territory was U. S. Marshal Crawley P. Dake, whose office was only a few blocks from Virgil; the next tier in the hierarchy was Yavapai County Sheriff Ed Bowers, whose office was in the county courthouse. The next layer of the law was represented by Prescott Village Marshal J. M. Dodson. Although Virgil was serving as constable, his job tended to have a bit more dignity than usual for that position, because Prescott was the territorial capital.

But not too much dignity. After all, lawmen dealt often with law breakers, and frequently these were low-lifes—drunks, tramps, cut-throats, swindlers, con-men, prostitutes, and opium peddlers. What each lawman could do was dictated by local and territorial law, and it did get confusing. For example, Virgil's predecessor as nightwatchman had also received the appointment of deputy

43

village marshal; this enabled him to make arrests, rather than just report mischief, burning saloons, and so forth.

In late 1878, U.S. Marshal Dake had to make Sheriff Bowers a deputy U. S. marshal; Dake needed help with federal prisoners. Dake had contracted with Yavapai County to house and feed certain prisoners, and he felt that the chain of command should include federal people. Therefore, Sheriff Bowers, a county official, was also Marshal Bowers, a federal lawman.[12]

Constable Virgil Earp did not get rich on the job. The position of night watchman had paid $75 a month. That of constable paid about the same, but there were more opportunities to earn extra. Constables, marshals, and sheriffs usually obtained fees when delivering summonses, transporting prisoners, collecting taxes, or issuing licenses to saloon keepers or prostitutes. There were also Constable Sales, where property was auctioned off in order to provide funds for unpaid debts; the constable in charge received a fee for handling the affair.

Where to put all the local rowdy types was solved in early September of 1878, when the Yavapai County Courthouse was completed. The building contained a jail, and the courthouse was "the finest building in Arizona," according to the *Miner*. The U. S. marshal, the sheriff of Yavapai County, the marshal of the Village of Prescott, and Prescott Precinct Constable Virgil Earp would use this new facility to house an assortment that ranged from drunks to stage robbers to wife beaters. There were never many prisoners on hand. For example, the *Enterprise* of March 22, 1879, indicated that several prisoners were in the County jail; three were U. S. convicts, and four were Territorial prisoners.

There is no record of any heroic deed performed by Virgil Earp while serving either as nightwatchman or as precinct constable in Prescott. It may have been because as a territorial capital, Prescott had more law and order than most cities of that size. Several companies and troops of the U. S. Army were also stationed at Whipple Barracks, but that did not necessarily mean more law and order. Frontier soldiers were notorious saloon wreckers, bar-room fighters, and debt malingerers.

There were the more mundane things to do: arrest a vagrant, who had no place to sleep; follow up a report on three youngsters seen gathering by the grocer's fence; investigate the larger than normal amount of smoke coming from Mrs. Jones' chimney; crack down on the local Chinese opium den; transport a horse thief from the jail to territorial court. Perhaps the following is typical of the duties of Prescott lawmen in this era:

> James Dodson, city marshal, found a mule tied
> to a post in front of Bones & Spencer, on the 1st
> day of December, and placed the same at the Gray
> Eagle Stable for safe keeping. The owner can have
> the same by paying stable bill.[13]

Two brief notices that appeared in the *Enterprise* of October 5, 1878, while Virgil had been acting as nightwatchman, give some feeling for the job, and his reputation:

> Mr. Earp arrested a man last night for shooting
> on the street.

> Some good shooting was done at the gallery,
> yesterday, the best scores being made by Charley
> Spencer, and Mr. Earp, each making 44, out of a
> possible 45.

This type of publicity might be one of the reasons there was so little trouble on the beat for Nightwatchman or Constable Earp.

His key role in the deadly Prescott shootout, coupled with news stories like the above, were bound to make drunks and trouble-makers careful in his presence.

The legal records for this era of Yavapai County history are fairly complete, and they indicate that Virgil Earp, a man of the law, was personally involved in two legal cases.

The first case actually consisted of two intertwined criminal cases in mid-1879: Territory vs. Henry T. Crum, and Territory vs. Virgil Earp. Crum, a stockraiser, lived at Oaks and Willows, and in September he noticed men from the Prescott and Mojave Stage Company digging a well on his land. He put on a pistol, grabbed a rifle, walked over and told them to get moving. He was arrested. The Grand Jury later refused to try Crum, and they also stated that they "have ignored the case and do not find any indictment against Virgil Earp."

Virgil's name does not appear anywhere in the case papers, so it is not known what role he played. At one point, Crum supposedly told the well-diggers to go get help if they felt like it, because he had his friends on hand. Perhaps Virgil was one of those backing Crum.

The case provides some interesting comments on the cost of doing law work in that era. Virgil's fellow constable, Frank Murray, was sent to arrest him on September 30. Constable Murray later presented the following bill to the court:

To arrest Earp	$2.00
Mileage, making arrest	2.40
2 subpoenas	1.00
Mileage, 26 miles	5.20

The other case was civil in nature, Robert Roggen vs. Virgil Earp, Case 649, Third District Court, June term of 1879. Roggen had been involved in a legal suit, and Constable Virgil Earp was ordered by Justice A. O. Noyes of the Prescott Precinct to seize some of Roggen's property to pay debts. Earp picked up three tons of corn, a bay horse, a wagon, and some harness. Virgil's defense was that he was carrying out the orders of Justice Noyes.

Territorial Justice Charles Silent ruled that what Virgil had seized was not all within the definition applying; he should not have taken the wagon and ordered its sale. Virgil was forced to return all goods to Roggen and pay court costs of $85.00. Such problems were apparently commonplace. Virgil's fellow constable, Frank Murray, got involved in a similar case in late 1879: James Glendenning vs. Frank Murray, in which Constable Murray, following justice court orders, got sued for removing more cattle than was required, because of a confusion in the justice court's stipulations.

During Virgil's years in Prescott, he continued to bring in a few extra dollars by providing firewood and lumber from his pine concession and sawmill west of town. The *Miner* of March 21, 1879, showed that he had bid to provide Fort Whipple with 500 cords of pine; the bid was accepted. Sometimes he had Allie give him a hand, even with lifting some of the heavier pieces. She finally rebelled, yelled, "Now lift it up yourself! I ain't no man," and stalked off to the house. This is the kind of give-and-take between Virgil and Allie Earp that permitted them to work out a reasonable relationship, although they both had strong personalities.[14]

Allie recalled another incident from this era that throws light on the couple's circumstances, as well as Virgil's attitude towards life. Virgil had just bought two new cows, and each cow had a calf. One morning, Virgil and his hired hand were working a crosscut saw, and Virgil told Allie to go and get the calves, as the men did not have time right then. Virgil, apparently with a wink to his

47

partner, told Allie to take a bell out to the field; the calves would think it was the cows, and follow her home:

> I didn't pay any attention to the wink and went out like he told me. . . .Finally I started ringin' that cowbell. The calves were layin' down behind one of the big boulders strewn all over. When they heard the bell they jumped up and ran at me. They almost knocked me down, buttin' like they did. Still ringin' the bell, I was so scared, I started runnin' and cryin' toward the corral with the calves tryin' to knock me down. Virge and the hired man stood laughin' fit to kill and wavin' their hats and shoutin' till I got inside.[15]

Near the end of this Prescott stay, Virgil became involved in a dispute. The *Miner* of October 3, 1879, reported that Frank Shultz arrived in town from near Thumb Butte "badly bruised about the head." According to Shultz, "Messrs. Earp and Hanson joined their forces and made an assault on him with a pistol and a large stick of wood." Shultz threatened to swear out an arrest warrant.

The *Miner* of October 24 mentioned that Shultz had discovered another rich gold mine to the west of town. A most likely interpretation of these scattered facts is that Shultz, a prospector-miner, roamed on Earp's sawmill concession at the base of Thumb Butte. He either prospected where he had no business, or he may have removed some pine from the Earp land. The justice and district court records for this period are complete, and contain no reference to Virgil being arrested or sued, so Shultz most likely decided to forget his head-bashing.

The Earps' time in Prescott was short now, as Tombstone

would soon beckon. But another personality must be introduced here, the nemesis of the Earps in Tombstone, one not overlooked by historians, but not given the crafty credit he should have received for events in that mining section. The man was Johnny Behan. And although historians of Tombstone and students of the famous October shootout know much about Behan, they tend to think of him in a role subservient to that of the Clantons or the McLaurys. Johnny Behan was not a giant among men, but among the crowd that he moved with in Tombstone, he was the most important. He was a Yavapai County man, and he and Virgil undoubtedly met dozens of times on the streets, in the saloons on Prescott's Whiskey Row, and on the stage routes of the county.

The Behan family, from Missouri, had come to this section of Arizona Territory in the mid-1860s, and Johnny Behan soon made a name for himself. He was an active small businessman, a Democratic politician, an inveterate office seeker, a back-slapper, a man known to all. He served two terms in the territorial legislature, once from Yavapai County, and later from Mohave County. He also held a string of Yavapai County jobs, including that of sheriff.[16]

In mid-1879 he got interested in the Tip Top District, bought a few mining claims and part of a store, and moved there in November, while keeping a residence in Prescott. Behan received one of the territory's few divorces, and his young son Albert resided with some of his father's many relatives in the Prescott home, and at other times with his mother.

One wonders: what kind of contact or relationship existed in Prescott between Virgil Earp and his to-be arch-foe, Johnny Behan? There is no handy record of business transaction, social intercourse, or legal contact between the two. Consider, for example, the following incident reported in the *Miner* of October 3, 1879:

> Hon. J. H. Behan had occasion to call at the
> Chinese laundry this P.M., when a controversy
> arose, leading to some half dozen of the pig-tail
> race making an assault on him with clubs. He tried
> to defend himself with a revolver, which, unfortu-
> nately, failed to work. He received several severe
> cuts about the head. Four of his assailants were
> arrested and lodged in jail.

Was Constable Virgil Earp on the scene? If not, he certainly heard the news about ex-Sheriff Behan's pulling out a worthless pistol while Chinese laundrymen made a laughing stock of him. In itself, the incident is instructive about frontier life, but events in Tombstone will later demonstrate that the laundry head-bashing was the type of confusing, gone-wrong incident that dogged Behan throughout much of his life.

In the middle of 1879, letters were exchanged among the widespread Earp family. Wyatt was getting bored in Dodge City, Morgan was in Montana but looking for something more exciting, Jim was jumping between Texas and Kansas and hoping for something steadier, and Virgil was in Arizona Territory, where he supposedly knew more than the other family members about the new, gloriously rich silver mining district of Tombstone, a few hundred miles to the southeast of Prescott.

Wyatt's biographer, Stuart Lake, attributes the Tombstone move to Virgil. Supposedly Virgil outlined a plan for the entire family—mining, running stages, opening a saloon, all in a city rich with miners and travelers of all sorts. Tombstone was to be the next big Western boom town, and the time to be there was now. Wyatt and Jim liked the sound of the word "silver," and because "Dodge's edge was getting dull," decided to move West.[17] The Dodge City *Globe* of September 9, 1879, reported:

> Wyatt Earp, the most efficient marshal Dodge
> City ever had, has resigned and is leaving for
> Arizona.

According to Allie, the above scenario never happened. Wyatt was indeed bored in Dodge, so he wrote to Virgil and suggested a Tombstone venture. Wyatt thought Jim and Morgan might also be interested. "Why shouldn't they all go and look over the new boom camp?"

Allie was furious upon reading the letter and said no to the Tombstone trip:

> Because we got a good home right here! That's
> why! We're too busy cuttin' wood to be traipsin'
> round the country![18]

Her opposition did her no good, as she learned what she had suspected when she first met Wyatt and Morgan in Dodge City. When the Earp boys gathered, there was a "silence, secrecy, and clannish solidarity," an attitude expressed by others who saw them together later in Tombstone.

One October day, a cry was sounded, the dog began to bark, and several wagons pulled into Virgil's yard in Prescott. Jim and Bessie Earp and daughter Hattie were in one wagon, and Wyatt and wife Mattie were in another. Wyatt also had brought along a string of horses to sell. Morg and his wife Lou would be joining them in weeks, and Doc Holliday and Big Nose Kate were also enroute, probably to spend the winter in Prescott before heading for Tombstone.[19]

Virgil quickly picked up the Tombstone enthusiasm, and within days they packed their belongings and sold out. This was particularly crushing for Allie, because Prescott had really been a

51

success for them. Virgil was selling some wood, had a fine job as constable; they owned a corral, some cows and calves, even a sewing machine. All this, and they had arrived a few years earlier with less than a dollar. Now, because of this Earp wanderlust, they would push aside security for the opportunity to hit bonanza in a distant mining town.

Before leaving Prescott, Virgil had one important piece of business to conduct. He walked into the office of U. S. Marshal Crawley P. Dake on November 27, 1879. There, he was officially commissioned a deputy U. S. marshal for Yavapai County; this would, in a few days, be amended in Tucson to indicate Pima County, where Tombstone was located.[20]

There has been too much speculation by Earp debunkers about why Virgil Earp received this appointment. Virgil was a local farmer-woodsman, who in addition had served well as a deputy sheriff, nightwatchman, and constable. He was a mature, responsible citizen, a physically tough, fearless fellow, a Civil War veteran, an experienced stage driver who had protected passengers, bullion bars, and the U. S. mail from unwanted incidents.

Furthermore, Dake's predecessor, U. S. Marshal Standefer, had been in charge of the posse in late 1877 that had rubbed out the trouble-makers Wilson and Tallos; Virgil had been the hero of that shootout. Dake, fairly new on the job, wanted a good man, his man, on the scene in Tombstone. That location was one of the fastest growing communities in the West, yet Dake, in faraway Prescott, did not have a loyal lieutenant there on the scene. Deputy U. S. Marshal Virgil W. Earp would be his contact in Tombstone.

The *Arizona Weekly Miner* of November 14, 1879, mentioned that Earp was about to leave for Tombstone, "just now the great center of attraction. We don't like tombstones, and shall avoid them so long as possible." The three Earp wagons—driven by

Virgil, Wyatt, and James—left Prescott in late November, figuring to arrive in Tombstone in a few weeks.

Among things left behind by Virgil was a debt, for $312 to the Goldwater Mercantile Company of Prescott, which the Goldwater family never pursued.[21]

Part of the local lore in Tombstone is that the Earps were carpet-baggers, come to town to bleed the miners, while decent folk had to work for a living. Decent folk—good, proper Arizonans like Johnny Behan.

The Behan-as-local-boy myth can be set aside quickly. In August of 1880, Behan ran for recorder at the Yavapai County Democratic convention and was soundly beaten [incumbent Wm. Wilkerson got 23 votes, Behan 9]. On August 20, Behan was bitter. The *Miner* quoted Behan as angry because the chairman "disregarded the conventional courtesy of naming him as Chairman of the Committee." The same issue reported on the treatment of Behan, the Tip Top delegate; the action against him was "an inexcusable breach of the common courtesy." In its news columns in the same issue, the *Miner* mentioned that Behan and his son Albert were headed back to their Tip Top home.

The above political embarrassment for Behan was of no great moment, but it highlights something not seen in the voluminous writings about Tombstone. Deputy U. S. Marshal Virgil W. Earp entered Tombstone in early December of 1879; on November 28th, the *Miner* had mentioned that "J. H. Behan has gone into business at Tiptop." A year later, Johnny Behan was still pining away hundreds of miles to the northwest of Tombstone in his Tip Top home, regretting that his erstwhile Yavapai County buddies had forsaken him. Johnny Behan, too, headed for Tombstone. But in his case it was less because he was attracted to the silver booming city; it was more because he was practically drummed out of the local political scene by his Democratic colleagues.

53

FOOTNOTES

1. Waters, *Earp Brothers*, p. 65.

2. Ibid., pp. 66-70.

3. A colorful, accurate, illustrated account of the era is Robert L. Spude, "A Land of Sunshine and Silver: Silver Mining in Central Arizona, 1871-1885," *Journal of Arizona History*, XVI (Spring, 1975), 29-76. For a more contemporary view, see John F. Blandy, "The Mining Region Around Prescott, Arizona," *Transactions, American Institute of Mining Engineers*, XI (1883), 286-91.

4. For other comments on this incident see the *Weekly Miner*, October 26, and the Prescott *Enterprise*, October 17, November 10, 1877.

5. *Weekly Miner*, April 12, 1878, for Gosper tour.

6. Ibid., October 1, October 11, 1878.

7. For smooth writing and fascinating interpretation, see Bert Fireman, "Fremont's Arizona Adventure," *American West*, I (Winter, 1964), 9-19.

8. *Enterprise*, August 3, 1878, has a detailed article entitled "Our New Marshal." See also Larry D. Ball, "Pioneer Lawman: Crawley P.Dake and Law Enforcement on the Southwestern Frontier," *Journal of Arizona History*, XIV (Autumn, 1973), 243-56. Gosper has not received the biography he deserves. The *Miner* of June 8, 1877, has an interesting article on him entitled "Hon. J. J. Gosper." He died, penniless, in a county facility in Los Angeles on May 14, 1913; obituary in Los Angeles *Times*, May 15, 1913, II, 1.

9. Federal census of 1880; I am thankful to Carl Chafin for pointing out this unusual Gosper/Holliday link.

10. *Enterprise*, September 4, October 9, 1878.

11. Ibid., November 9, 1878.
12. *Weekly Miner*, August 30, 1878.
13. Ibid., December 6, 1878.
14. Waters, *Earp Brothers*, p. 73.
15. Ibid., pp. 73-74.
16. I have a large Behan family file, largely culled from the files of the *Weekly Miner* and *Enterprise*. See also, Geo. H. Kelly (comp.), *Legislative History: Arizona, 1864-1912* (Tucson, 1926), p. 361 for a brief biography of Behan. The best article is Glenn Boyer, "Johnny Behan of Tombstone," *Frontier Times*, July, 1976, pp. 6-9, 55-57, although Boyer is not even-handed towards his subject.
17. Lake, *Wyatt Earp*, pp. 228-29.
18. Waters, *Earp Brothers*, p. 75.
19. Most of the comments on planning for Tombstone are based on Allie's reporting; Waters, *Earp Brothers*, pp. 74-80.
20. Copy in the Library, Arizona Historical Society, Tucson.
21. Note by Melissa Ruffner Weiner in Archives, Sharlot Hall Museum. Mrs. Weiner, a descendant of Sheriff Ruffner of Yavapai County, has written several histories of Prescott.

III: TO TOMBSTONE

In the last days of November, 1879, three Earp wagons left Prescott, bound for the silver bonanza of Tombstone. Virgil and Allie were in one wagon, Wyatt and Mattie Blaylock were in another, and James, wife Bessie, and her daughter Hattie were in the third. According to Allie, the wagons were fully loaded, as she did not intend to leave behind the few decent possessions she was able to get in the good recent years in Prescott, including her new sewing machine. Tied to some of the wagons were the small number of extra horses that Wyatt had brought out from Kansas. As with any frontier boom town, horses were in great demand, and even rundown animals commanded high prices in Tombstone.

The Earps traveled via Wickenburg, Phoenix, and Tucson. They camped overnight outside Tucson, the seat of Pima County; at that time, Pima County included Tombstone. Virgil visited with the deputy U. S. marshal stationed in Tucson and had his own commission altered; he was now a deputy U. S. marshal, with authority to act in Pima County.

On the rocky road to Tombstone, the Earp party had an incident. Virgil's wagon was in the lead, and looking backwards he could see Wyatt and Jim's wagons at the edge of the road, almost in the ditch. They had moved aside to allow the Benson-bound stage to go by. Virgil also moved to the side, in spite of Allie's warning that he might put them in the ditch. Virgil yelled, "We got to get over. The U.S. mail has got the right to the road over everybody. Nothin' can stop it."

The stage came zooming by, not slowing a whit, and the vehicle scraped Virgil's wagon, making one of the horses bleed. The stage driver "give us a laugh, and the stage rattled off in a cloud of dust."

The man had indeed riled Virgil, who "laid on his whip," and his outfit chased after the speedy stage. Wyatt and Jim, not knowing exactly what had happened, followed as quickly as they could in their wagons.

Five miles down the road, the stage stopped at a station to change horses. The driver was standing around, jawing with the passengers, when Virgil drove up. Virgil knocked the driver down; he got up, and was smashed down again. There commenced a fist fight, "Virge just thumped the puddin' out of him, knockin' him down as fast as he could get up." By this time Wyatt and Jim had joined, but there was no need for them to participate. The driver apologized, probably seeing for the first time, on the chest of his powerful six-feet-one opponent, the badge of a deputy U. S. marshal.[1]

By this time the party was only about forty miles from Tombstone, and Allie, having witnessed the bloody fistfight, did not have good thoughts about their new home, a feeling not helped by the name of the new settlement.

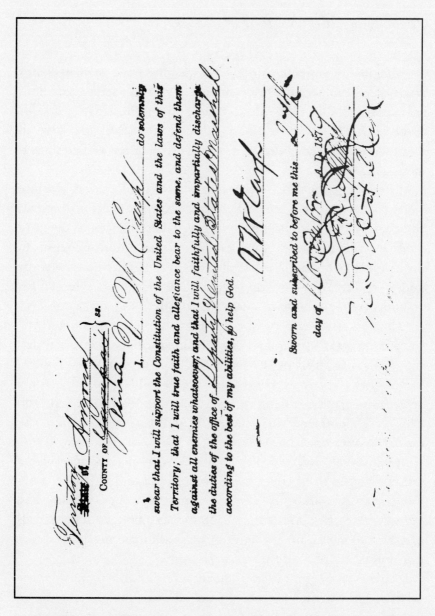

When Virgil Earp arrived in Tombstone in late November of 1879 he was carrying the authority of a Deputy U. S. Marshal. This is his oath of office. Fred Dodge Collection, Huntington **Library**

Various documents and court testimony have the Earp party arriving in Tombstone on December 1, 1879, but such a date does not seem possible; the group was still in Prescott as late as November 27. However, there is no doubt that they were in Tombstone by December 9, when the Earp brothers signed several mining claims.[2]

Tombstone and the Earp brothers have been subject to quite a literary barrage over the years, and the history of the settlement, and that of the famous shootout, are covered in some detail in other studies. However, some comment on Tombstone seems in order, and although this is not the saga of the Earp brothers, some understanding of the relationship among the clan is essential for an appreciation of this well-known frontier era.

Civilian scout and prospector Ed Schieffelin discovered the silver deposits in the summer of 1877, and the name "Tombstone" was chosen as an irony; he had been told, probably by scout Al Sieber, that all he would find in the area would be his tombstone. Schieffelin proved otherwise, and soon he, his brother Al, and Dick Gird confirmed that the silver deposits were among the richest in Western America.[3]

Only a well-used word like "boom" can give the measure of the rapid growth of the mining community and all those other things that go with it—stores, stage lines, churches, schools, and saloons. The town population by 1880 was 2,000, with thousands of others living in surrounding sites, especially at mills and mines in Contention, Millville, and Charleston.

Silver, although a precious metal, is unlike gold in many ways. Gold is unique in that it is isolated, usually existing as an independent element. It may be in quartz, or in other country [host] rock, but it is still gold. Furthermore, gold is often found separated from its host rock; these gold deposits are "placers," such as nuggets, flour gold, and flakes, found in gravels, stream

First and foremost, Tombstone was a silver mining and milling town. This is the hoisting works at Contention Mill. Arizona Quarterly Illustrated, April, 1881

beds, hillsides, and so forth. Gold placer deposits can be located and worked with crude tools and good eyes. Pan, rocker, and long tom were enough to wrest fortunes from Western placer deposits.

Alas, there is little silver in nature that is so cooperative as to lie in a stream bed or on the surface and sparkle for the interested prospector. Silver quickly associates, that is combines, with other elements and is never found in paying quantities as an isolated element. That presents two problems: it is practically impossible to spot silver by looking at it, and it is always difficult to separate silver from its many mineral associations.

Almost every ore of silver was mined at Tombstone. A leading ore there was argentite [the Latin word for silver is *argentum*], which is a silver sulphide. Other important Tombstone silver ores were cerargyrite or horn silver; cerussite, a silver and lead combination; and galena, bromyrite, pyrargyrite, proustite, and other ores. The ore mined at Tombstone from 1879 through 1933 produced 81% silver, 14% gold, and 5% lead, copper, manganese, and zinc. Silver, of course, is a fantastic conductor, and takes a very high polish, once it has been separated from the other elements. Therefore, the metal has significant practical as well as aesthetic attributes.

Because silver is what it is, a silver camp never resembles a gold camp in its initial stages. There is no room in a silver camp for the small operator. Ores must first be crushed, then treated with chemicals to reduce or remove all the unwanted elements and gangue, or "country rock." Therefore, Tombstone was no Sutter's Creek, La Paz, Nome, or Cripple Creek. From the first, mills and processing plants were the order of the day, and hundreds of companies were formed. Huge pieces of machinery were brought in from Los Angeles and San Francisco, and engineers and mill supervisors were hired from throughout the West. The capital requirements, therefore, were different from those of a placer gold operation, as was the labor supply. Yet, there were fortunes to be made—in the hills, in the companies that were formed, and in the saloons, hotels, and other merchant houses that saw to the provisioning and care of the large mining population.[4]

The original plan of the Earps was to get in on the ground floor of the new community; Wyatt in particular wanted to open a stage line, and Virgil was "earmarked" for the law. James was supposed to do what he always did—operate a gaming house and push liquor. Well, the Earps were early on the scene, but not early enough. Several well-established stage lines already fed Tombstone, and Wyatt saw at once that he needed to develop other ways to get money.

One of the first things the Earps did was what most newcomers did—they filed a few mining claims. Each brother went his separate way on a few deals, but on most of the dozen or so claims they filed in 1879-80, Virgil, Wyatt, and James were part of the claimant list, usually with Robert "Uncle Bob" Winders, a well-known Fort Worth saloon man who had been early on the Tombstone scene. They filed their first claim on December 9, 1879, and by mid-1880 owned the Mountain Maid, Earp, Grasshopper, Mattie Blaylock, and Rocky Ridge. None of these claims was distinguished in any way, but the Earps made some money eventually by selling them to other dreamers.[5]

Upon arriving in Tombstone, the Earps were uneasy. Most good claims were already taken up, there was no stage line future as they had hoped, and good jobs were hard to find. The boys "kept their eyes open," claimed Allie, although Virgil was the only real worker in the family. Wyatt wasn't interested in chopping wood or in anything that might disturb "them long slender hands of his." James, with a gimpy shoulder from a Civil War bullet, couldn't do physical labor. Virgil did a few odd jobs, but nothing steady seemed in the offing for the Earps.[6]

Allie brightened considerably when she found a use for the new sewing machine that she had insisted on bringing from Prescott. She and Wyatt's wife Mattie had, as their first paying job, to make a huge canvas tent for a new saloon. That led to other sewing jobs, and at least some money was available. Soon Jim got a job dealing faro, and Wyatt was hired as a Wells, Fargo stage guard. The Earps, who had all been rooming together in cramped quarters, found separate housing. Virgil and Allie moved to a house on the southwest corner of First and Fremont, and Wyatt and Mattie lived on the northeast corner; Jim and Bessie were just a block away. Although privacy was important, Earps did not like to be too far away from each other.[7]

The year 1880 brought to town many personalities that were to figure prominently in the exciting months ahead: John Clum, George W. Parsons, Johnny Behan, Fred Dodge, Doc Holliday, and Morgan Earp.

Clum arrived early in the year to start a newspaper, appropriately entitled the *Epitaph*, which was backed financially by mining executive Richard Gird. Clum, although an Easterner, was no novice. He had served as an Indian Agent with the San Carlos Apaches and had edited newspapers in Tucson, and more recently, in Florence, Arizona Territory. He would become an Earp booster until his death half a century later.[8]

George Whitwell Parsons, an educated bank clerk most recently from San Francisco, arrived with mining intentions and facile pen; Parsons, who was to know intimately most of the Tombstone figures, recorded hundreds of events and biographical comments in one of the most valuable series of diaries in any Western community.[9]

Behan, having been dismissed by his Yavapai colleagues as a Democrat out-of-favor, arrived in late summer, hoping, as always, to get a few political appointments—anything to avoid work. He made a small investment in a stable with Thomas Dunbar and waited for his chance.[10]

Doc Holliday, who had long shown a lack of interest in dentistry, had floated across the West from Dodge City, hitting gambling halls in Albuquerque, Santa Fe, and spent the winter in Prescott, living in the same quarters as Territorial Secretary John Gosper. Doc had done well at the Prescott tables and was eager to work the faro games in Tombstone. Furthermore, Wyatt Earp was in Tombstone; Doc and Wyatt had become dedicated pals in Dodge City, and Doc was looking to renew the friendship. This would be done, but to Wyatt's regret.[11]

Two other people who arrived shortly after Virgil and Wyatt were Fred Dodge and Morgan Earp. Dodge had been sent out from the San Francisco office of Wells, Fargo to work as an undercover agent. Stage robberies and other peculiar goings-on had disturbed the company, and they sent their best field man to investigate secretly, while posing as a gambler and man-about-town. Morgan Earp, younger than Virgil and Wyatt, had been serving as a policeman in Montana and decided to throw in with his brothers in Arizona Territory.

Fred Dodge wrote that when he arrived in Tombstone, "I carefully looked around and I saw two men who were carefully sizing me up—It was plain to be seen that they were Brothers and that they were outstanding Men." Puzzled, Dodge became even more apprehensive when the two men started towards him. "My Name is Wyatt Earp," and Dodge replied, "My name is Fred Dodge." Wyatt then introduced the bemused Dodge to his brother Virgil.

The explanation of this strange encounter was Fred Dodge's appearance. To Wyatt and Virgil, Fred Dodge was a dead ringer for their brother Morgan, whom they were expecting. In fact, as Virgil, Wyatt, and Fred Dodge started walking down the street,

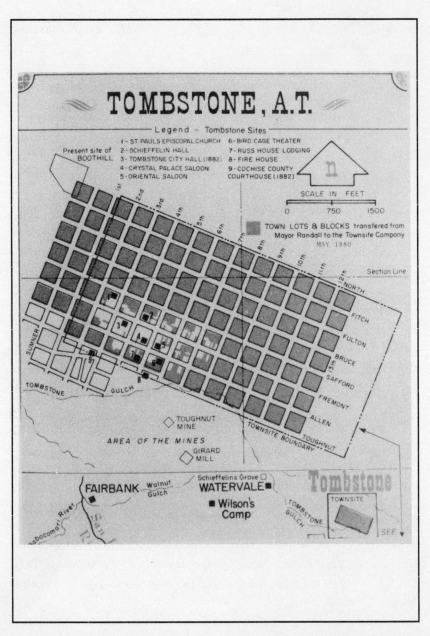

Main streets and buildings of historic Tombstone, when that mining community was in full swing. Don Bufkin Map, Arizona & the West, Spring, 1979

they heard a comment: "There is another one of the Earp Boys."

Morgan arrived a few weeks later, and Fred Dodge and Morgan agreed with the assessment—they looked almost like twins. They were frequently mistaken for each other, a fact they found hilarious after a while, as they decided to room together, making it difficult even for acquaintances to tell them apart.[12]

Fred Dodge remained true to his Wells, Fargo undercover task, never leaking a word, even to the Earps, that he was a detective. Dodge got in touch with company general manager John Valentine, and soon the San Francisco office hired Wyatt Earp as shotgun messenger and guard on the various bullion runs out of Tombstone. Fifty years later Dodge had not wavered from his decision, as he wrote in a letter of 1928: "That my judgment was good in this Selection was proven in many ways by future Events."[13]

There were changes in the air, and in the talk, in Tombstone and in Pima County. Tombstone was growing rapidly, and many residents felt it was not being well served by the distant county seat in Tucson. Agitation began in 1880 to create a separate county, which accelerated as the year drew to a close.[14]

Meanwhile, James was dealing faro, and Wyatt was riding shotgun for Wells, Fargo, but Virgil—aside from Allie's sewing—did not have much money coming in. He did some work on the mining claims, and he also earned a few dollars as deputy U. S. marshal. In one incident in March of 1880, Virgil cracked a counterfeiting scheme in Tombstone and confiscated the plates and dies. The prisoner—C. S. Hogan—escaped from jail, a circumstance that Virgil would grow to know better in the coming year.[15]

A notice in the *Arizona Weekly Miner* of July 30, 1880, shows another example of Virgil's assignment and that he continued to be Territorial Marshal Dake's eyes in this part of Arizona:

> A dispatch received this morning from Deputy
> U.S. Marshal Earp, says that the people of Tomb-
> stone have notified the Chinamen in that vicinity
> that they must leave, and that a riot is threatened
> if they do not go.
> The above dispatch was received by U. S.
> Marshal Dake.

While it is true that Virgil was a deputy U. S. marshal, most law enforcement was in the hands of local officials, which included the sheriff of Pima County, and the village marshal of Tombstone. Virgil was called in when federal questions arose, such as border problems, robbing of the U. S. Mails, or when posses were needed that crossed various law enforcement jurisdictions.

Law enforcement in Tombstone, and in this part of Pima County, was collapsing in 1880. The new population was growing beyond expectations, and all sorts of people had moved in to profit from the situation. Gamblers, prostitutes, confidence men of all sorts were arriving in droves, along with stock-jobbers and other kinds of paper-cheaters that afflicted the mining frontiers.

The newness of the town was complicated by a confusing land situation. Original Tombstone had actually been 100 yards to the south, on the site of the Wide Side Mine. Because of mining needs there, and flatter land elsewhere, the Tombstone Townsite Company was formed. The firm sold lots in a new "Tombstone," which became the Tombstone known to history. However, the whole business of selling lots, filing claims, and lot-jumping became more critical in Tombstone than in most other Western towns. The fact that the town had moved, coupled with an ineffective police and county law enforcement capability, meant that certain people were pushing other people around.

The complicated townsite squabble must at least be summarized here, because many of the principals figured in subsequent Tombstone events. The village mayor, Alder Randall, was actually the tool of James Clark and Mike Gray, who had gained control of the company. Without patents, and without deeds, the firm of Clark, Gray & Co., with the connivance of Mayor Randall, would try to force Tombstone residents to pay rent on land of questioned ownership. Among the leaders protesting this high-handed move were Editor John Clum, Deputy U. S. Marshal Virgil Earp, Attorney Wells Spicer, and Robert "Uncle Bob" Winders, who was co-claimant with Virgil in several mining claims. An even more telling combination was that Gray's son, Dixie Lee, was in cahoots with the Clanton gang; he would meet his death in a cattle rustling blood bath on the Mexican border.[16]

Diarist George Parsons put some of the flavor of the times about lots and lot jumping on paper. His entry for February 17, 1880:

> Model town. Shooting this a.m., and two fellows in afternoon attempted to go for one another with guns and six shooters, but friends interposed. . . .Mingled with the hardy miners tonight. Talk of killing indulged in again tonight. Everyone goes heeled. Jumping claims great cause of trouble.[17]

Part of his entry for May 10, 1880:

> Bad state of feeling in town tonight and throughout day. Shooting and rows of various kinds. Lots being jumped the trouble.

During Wyatt's months as Wells, Fargo guard, he had no

business. That is, no real problems erupted on the dusty trails while he had shotgun and pistol handy. His shotgun-riding tour ran from January through July, which gave Wells, Fargo considerable satisfaction, and also impressed the sheriff of Pima County, Charlie Shibell, who made Wyatt a deputy sheriff. The *Epitaph* printed the following on October 20, 1880:

> The appointment of Wyatt Earp as Deputy Sheriff by Sheriff Shibell, is an eminently proper one, and we, in common with the citizens generally, congratulate the latter on his selection. Wyatt has filled various positions in which bravery and determination were requisites, and in every instance proved himself the right man in the right place.[18]

Fred Dodge did what he considered the only sensible thing—he secretly arranged to have his friend and room-mate Morgan Earp replace Wyatt as the new Wells, Fargo messenger-guard.

By autumn of 1880, therefore, the Earps were settled, and well connected in Tombstone. Virgil was the deputy U. S. marshal; Wyatt was deputy sheriff of Pima County; Morgan was the Wells, Fargo guard; and James was busy dealing faro.

Furthermore, they had gradually earned the admiration and support of the *Epitaph* editor, John Clum. The Earp brothers had been long-established Republicans—Wyatt had been a state delegate in Kansas—and Clum was the leader of the local Republican faction. This partisan factor, plus their liking for each other, made Clum and the Earps go through the troubled times together.

To say that the Earps were not universally well-liked would cause guffaws in Arizona, even to this day. Two broad coalitions evolved in the tense period of 1880-82, and to this day historians,

Arizonans, and lovers of the West agree that there were two groups, but agree on little else, such as membership, motivation, criminal intent, or degree of community backing of each group. But some attempt at defining these two factions must be made in order to make some sense out of the confrontations and chaos that would emerge.

The thousands of people in Tombstone and environs had to eat, and in a desert, feeding so many people is no easy task. However, meat was a desired commodity, and there were ranchers and cowboys in the vicinity willing to provide the cattle. The only problem was that this part of rural Arizona was thinly settled, with nowhere near enough livestock for Tombstone needs. Yet, the Mexican border was not far away, and cattle rustling became big business almost overnight.

Some of this cattle stealing was done by typical rustlers; yet some of the smaller ranchers in Pima County seem to have taken to these Mexican excursions also, to supplement their incomes and to get a slice of the new silver action in Tombstone. Many of the agricultural types in southern Arizona were Texan, and the Texas cowboy types dominated the lifestyle in this part of the frontier.

In the 1870s and 1880s, in Arizona and California, the word "cowboy" had only one meaning, a rustler who was also a trouble-maker, a wild sort bent on thieving and a good time. William Henry Bishop, a correspondent from *Harper's Magazine*, visited Tombstone, and clarified that "cowboys" had originally been cowboys, but by then [c. 1881] as a class "become stealers of cattle." There were still some legitimate cowboys, but the easy money from rustling gave the entire group a new reputation:

> The cow-boys frequenting Tombstone at this
> time were generally from ranches in the San Pedro
> and San Simon valleys. There were said to be

strongholds in the San Simon Valley for concealing stolen cattle, until rebranded and prepared for market, where no officer of the law ever ventured. The running off of stock from Mexico was possibly looked upon only as a more dashing form of smuggling, although it was marked by frequent tragedies on both sides.[19]

This happy-go-lucky, or "free spirit" attitude went on because the U. S. Army could not get involved in anything resembling police work, and the thinly scattered officers of the law couldn't cope with the large number of cowboys. But the "free spirit" times were coming to an end. There were bloody incidents at the Mexican border, which led to hot telegraph exchanges between Washington, D.C., Prescott, and Tombstone. The cowboys had gotten out of hand, blustering around Tombstone, Charleston, and other local sites, and had even taken to grabbing local stockmen's cattle, horses, and mules.

There is no cowboy "roster," but prominent frontier types who were part of this group included Johnny Ringo, Curly Bill [Wm. Brocius], and the Clanton and McLaury families.[20]

After he arrived in Tombstone in the summer of 1880, Johnny Behan quickly looked for various power blocks and settled on the cowboy faction as the one to cultivate. He became very friendly with them on their town visits, played faro at the same table, and seemed to have enjoyed their company; he would later room with Johnny Ringo.

The cowboy scourge cannot be overemphasized. Writers critical of the Earps maintain that the cowboy threat was never really a problem, just a few wild Texas cowboys shooting up a saloon or so. Governor Fremont's territorial address in February of 1881 opened with an assessment of the border problems, the threat to life and property on both sides of the line, and the need to "break up and destroy the organized bands of outlaws which now infest that region."[21] Even Legislator Thomas Dunbar of Tombstone, no friend of the Earps, was quoted in the *Arizona Weekly Miner* of March 4, 1881, as saying that the "Cow Boys are making it warm for stock men in Southern Arizona."

Another person who arrived in town sometime in 1880 was Josephine "Sadie" Marcus, eighteen-year-old daughter of San Francisco merchant Henry Marcus. According to Bat Masterson, who knew her well, Sadie was one of the many working girls in the Tombstone saloons, one of the better looking, high-class types. Johnny Behan took a liking to her, and soon she was living with Behan and his young son Albert.[22]

The chronology is not clear, but it is known that soon Sadie Marcus met Wyatt Earp, and without too much hesitation, she dumped Behan for Wyatt. This not only embarrassed Behan, but it infuriated him. He could never challenge Wyatt face-to-face, for reasons which will become clear, but the dumping festered and would be one of many factors which made him a bitter Earp antagonist.[23]

There were two newspapers in Tombstone, and Clum's *Epitaph* was solidly behind the mine owners and the Earp brothers. The *Nugget*, edited by Territorial Delegate [a Democrat] Harry Woods, gradually backed the cowboy faction.

Before throwing more factors into this Tombstone cauldron, it might be well to see how these groups fell into place:

EARPS	COWBOYS
Townsmen/miners/law & order	Rural, ranchers
Epitaph	*Nugget*
Clum/businessmen	Behan
Republicans	Democrats
Midwesterners/Easterners	Southerners/Texans

The first encounter that led to bitterness between the cowboys and the Earps happened in July and August of 1880. Six government mules were stolen from the U.S. Army at Camp Rucker. Lieutenant Joseph Hurst was charged with getting the animals returned. A posse was formed consisting of Hurst and four soldiers, Deputy U. S. Marshal Virgil Earp, Wyatt and Morgan Earp, and Wells, Fargo agent Marshall Williams. They tracked the stolen mules to the McLaury ranch, but Lieutenant Hurst worked out a deal whereby the mules would be returned, but no action would be taken against anyone. The Earps were disgusted and returned to Tombstone. [The mules never were returned.] A few weeks later, Hurst saw Wyatt in Tombstone:

> Hurst cautioned me and my brothers, Virgil
> and Morgan, to look out for those men, as they had
> made some threats against our lives.[24]

On the evening of October 27, 1880, a shooting occurred which would have many ramifications for Tombstone and the Earps. The cowboys were in town carousing, drinking too much, and getting out of hand. Soon, shots rang out amid loud shouting and yelling. Several cowboys, including Curly Bill [Brocius], were out in the street banging away at the moon or stars. What they didn't know was that Village Marshal Fred White was watching them. He went up to Curly Bill and said, "I am an officer; give me your pistol."[25]

Meanwhile, Wyatt Earp, deputy sheriff of Pima County, had been in Billy Owen's Saloon a block away and heard the shots. Wyatt ran out of the saloon, saw brother Morgan and asked him for a pistol. Morgan did not have one but pointed to Fred Dodge a few steps ahead. With Dodge's pistol in hand Wyatt ran to the scene of the ruckus just as Curly Bill had drawn his pistol out of his holster. Marshal White grabbed the barrel, but Curly Bill wouldn't let go. Wyatt threw his arms around Curly Bill, and Marshal White, encouraged by the help, yelled:

Now, you G____ d_____ s____ of a b_____, give up that pistol.

Unfortunately, White jerked the pistol further, and it went off, blasting Marshal White in the stomach. Wyatt "buffaloed" Curly Bill, that is, cracked him over the skull with his pistol, threw him to the ground, and placed him under arrest. White, fatally wounded, lasted until the next day. Before he died he gave some details of the encounter, exonerated Curly Bill from any serious crime, saying the shooting was accidental.

A hearing in late December in Tucson before Justice of the Peace Joseph Neugass, saw a parade of witnesses, including Wyatt and Morgan Earp, some friends of Curly Bill, and a few curious onlookers. All reported basically the same tale of a confused frontier incident, and Curly Bill was released without being charged in Marshal White's death.[26]

The incident certainly reinforced the existing ill-feeling between the cowboys and the Earps. Wyatt had bashed Curly Bill's skull, arrested him, and humiliated him in front of friends and strangers, a grievance not soon forgotten by Curly Bill. More important, though, was that the Tombstone village marshal was dead. White had been young Tombstone's first village marshal, and the inexperienced common council was in near panic.

Mayor Alder Randall and the Tombstone Common Council met on October 28, the day of Marshal White's death, and appointed Virgil W. Earp the assistant village marshal of Tombstone. The Mayor was also authorized to:

> Issue a Proclamation stating that hereafter Ordinance No. 9 against carrying concealed weapons be strictly enforced.[27]

This move placed the Earp brothers in the forefront of doings in the boom town. Wyatt was still serving as deputy sheriff of Pima County, and Virgil, in addition to being a deputy U. S. marshal was now also assistant village marshal.

But this appointment was not to be the fulfilling event that the Earps had anticipated. Virgil's appointment was only temporary. The common council called a special election for village marshal to be held on November 12. Six officers were to arrange the election, all "under the command of Assistant Marshal Virgil Earp."[28]

The election was held, but the results were not pleasing to Virgil and the Earps. Ben Sippy, a do-nothing, harmless, pleasant fellow polled 311 votes, to Virgil's 259. Sippy would fill out White's term, and a new election would be held early in January.[29]

Disappointed with the results, Virgil decided not to be second to Sippy, and on November 15 the common council accepted his resignation, giving him $54.83 for his two week's work. The Earps may have been bubbling to the surface, but it was difficult to stay at the top.

Another political rhubarb during this month involved Wyatt. On November 9, 1880, he resigned as deputy sheriff of Pima County. His place as deputy sheriff was taken by Johnny Behan. Wyatt had been caught in a bind. He had received his appointment from Sheriff Charlie Shibell and had done yeoman work in the far-flung county for some months. However, in the election in Pima County scheduled for November 17, Shibell was running against Wyatt's friend, Bob Paul. Wyatt did not campaign openly for Paul, yet he owed his position to Shibell. His resignation, he hoped, would show that he was not taking sides in the election. It goes without saying that Wyatt was not happy being replaced by Behan, but that was Shibell's choice, not his.

In the November 17 election, Shibell beat out Paul by the slim margin of 42 votes. Howls and complaints were soon heard, as it was revealed that sparsely settled rural districts had produced more votes than there were cattle. In particular, Ike Clanton, the loudest-mouthed of that family, was said to have stuffed the ballot box in San Simon Valley; Ike had been designated as election inspector, and Johnny Ringo an election judge, which says much about the thinking of the citizens of the San Simon Valley. A recount was ordered by the territorial court. The *Arizona Daily Star* of January 20 reported that of the 104 votes cast in San Simon, 100 were fraudulent. On January 27, 1881, it was announced that the new sheriff of Pima County was Bob Paul.[30]

Two other well-known Western figures came to town in January and February—Bat Masterson and Luke Short. These two sporting types from Dodge City had been closely associated there with Wyatt Earp. Bat had been a law officer with Dodge City and Ford County and looked to Wyatt as a mentor. Luke Short had run several gaming places in Dodge, and had been in business with Wyatt at two different locations. By this time Wyatt owned some of the action [one-quarter] at Tombstone's Oriental Saloon, so he

77

Dake, as U.S. Marshal, was the leading law enforcement official in the Arizona Territory. He appointed Virgil Earp as Deputy U.S. Marshal. Arizona Historical Society

got positions for Masterson and Short there. Neither took a great liking for Tombstone and left in a few months. The only thing of interest Bat did was to join in a posse and witness a street fight.

Meanwhile, a whole new system of government was being pushed for Tombstone—city status, with a clean slate of officers. With George Parsons as campaign manager, the Law and Order League nominated John Clum for mayor of the city-to-be; the Earps were prominent members of this faction. Much of Clum's support came from Tombstone residents who resented the Tombstone Townsite Company, and Clum had led the fight against that tainted firm. On January 4 of 1881, in the first election for the new city, Clum's party won out, and the *Epitaph* editor was now also Mayor Clum. No such good fortune followed the rest of the ticket. Virgil Earp, again a candidate, lost for the second time to the incumbent marshal, Ben Sippy.[31]

Political complications were getting even more complex. In the closing months of 1880, the push to create a new county centering on Tombstone was on, led by local Democrats Thomas Dunbar and Harry Woods, both members of the legislature. It was widely acknowledged throughout the Territory that such a county would be created. Naturally, patronage would be available, and many stood in line to grasp at chances for office.[32]

Foremost among the graspers were Wyatt Earp and Johnny Behan. Both men figured they had a good chance to become sheriff of the new county, which would provide a handsome income based on tax collection fees, fees for transporting and housing criminals, the providing of various licenses, and so forth. Wyatt had had a respectable lawman career in Dodge City, a career which was known to all, and he had served well as a Wells, Fargo guard and as deputy sheriff of Pima County. Behan had had many political offices in Mohave and Yavapai counties, had served two terms in the Legislature, and had also been sheriff of Yavapai County.

So far as political power went, there were more questions than answers. Governor Fremont was a Republican; Territorial Secretary Gosper was a Republican; U. S. Marshal Dake was a Republican; Wyatt Earp was a Republican. On the other hand, candidate Behan was a Democrat, seemingly without much chance of receiving the sheriff's appointment.

The above simplified view was shredded by back-door infighting. Fremont and Gosper, the two leading officials in the Territory, both Republicans, despised each other. Gosper pulled every trick he could in Washington to get Fremont removed so that the people of Arizona Territory would have an active, concerned governor, that is, himself. Fremont knew this and avoided contact with Gosper—easy to do, as Fremont was seldom in the Territory. It was also well-known in Prescott that Gosper had spent the winter months palling around with Doc Holliday, one of the Earp crowd.

The *Arizona Miner*, as the main newspaper in the territorial capital, also carried influence beyond its size. Editor Beach, who had been a staunch supporter of Gosper, changed sides and began to accuse Gosper of everything from womanizing to gambling to feeding at the public trough. Anything related to Gosper, then—such as an Earp appointment—was bound to get a bad press in Prescott.

The *Miner* had long been a supporter of Behan when he had resided in Yavapai County, and stuck with him now. By late January of 1881, the *Miner* reported:

> It seems evident that the new county of
> Cochise will be formed, and in this connection the
> MINER would respectfully ask that John H. Behan
> be appointed the first Sheriff of what is to be one

80

of the most important counties in the Territory. .
He has been tried in this county as Sheriff and
never found wanting.

One can imagine the pressures on Fremont. The new county
would be created. The position of sheriff was the most important
office in the new county. By appointing Earp he would be keeping
true to Republican practice; yet, Earp was Gosper's man. Furthermore, the local [Prescott] *Miner* was pushing Behan, and although
Behan was a Democrat, his appointment would at least lead to
some praise for Fremont in the *Miner*.[33]

Wyatt began to sense that things were not going his way.
Shortly before the Legislature was to act in creating the new
county, Wyatt went to Behan for a council of war. He claimed that
he and Behan had reached an understanding. Behan would
become sheriff, and his first duty would be to appoint Wyatt as
deputy sheriff. They would then slice up the various pies, such as
tax collection fees, license costs, and so forth.[34]

On February 3, 1881, the legislature passed enabling legisla-
tion for the new County of Cochise, and Governor Fremont signed
it the same day. On February 11, the *Miner* announced:

John H. Behan, Yavapai's old Sheriff, has been
appointed by Governor Fremont, Sheriff of Cochise
county. A good selection to the very core. John has
been tried and never found wanting.

Wyatt never heard from Behan about the deputyship. In fact,
within weeks of Behan's appointment, Behan named Harry
Woods, editor of the *Nugget* and a Democratic member of the
legislature, deputy sheriff of Cochise County.

Clum was outraged by all of this. Here he had created a Law

and Order League, swept the rascals out, and a month after he became mayor, the governor had selected Democrats rather than Republicans for the Cochise County positions. The *Miner* by this time was overjoyed, plugging Behan, ridiculing Clum and his complaints, and writing that Governor Fremont had made a great choice. The melon would be sliced in the new County of Cochise by Democrats.[35]

A further incident in January of 1881 indicated how law and order was continuing to break down in the Tombstone vicinity. In nearby Charleston, chief engineer Philip Schneider of the Corbin Mill, in a saloon, accused Johnny-Behind-The-Deuce [Michael O'Rourke] of robbing his cabin. After an exchange of insults, which carried over into the street, Schneider continued to taunt the "Deuce," who pulled out his pistol and shot Schneider, who died almost instantly. Constable George McKelvey arrested "Deuce" and escorted him to Tombstone in a buckboard.

What happened next is only conjecture, as legends and exaggerations abound. According to Wyatt biographers, in Tombstone an angry mob gathered, especially miners, intent on lynching "Deuce." Wyatt, single-handedly, held them at bay with shotgun and steely eyes. Actually, there is no contemporary proof that Wyatt Earp was even on hand. The best contemporary account was by George Parsons, who recorded in his diary that "Many of the miners armed themselves and tried to get at the murderer. Several times, yes a number of times, rushes were made and rifles leveled, causing Mr. Stanley and me to get behind the most available shelter."[36] But, Parsons pointed out, the officers of the law prevailed and took their man to Tucson.

The *Epitaph* of January 17 did state that an ugly crowd was gathering, but an armed posse was there to prevent "any attempt on the part of the crowd to lynch the prisoner." The *Epitaph* mentioned by name U. S. Deputy Marshal Virgil Earp, Pima County

Deputy Sheriff Johnny Behan, and City Marshal Ben Sippy.
Johnny-Behind-The-Deuce was taken to Tucson, but he escaped
from jail and never again surfaced.

The boldness of bandits became more evident on the night of
March 15, 1881, a few miles out of town. The Benson stage was
attacked by from four to eight men, guns blasting away. They had
not counted on the presence of fearless Bob Paul, riding shotgun.
The driver, Budd Philpot, had been sick, so Paul had changed
places with him. Paul, a giant of a man and without fear of any
other, held the reins in one hand and kept blasting back at the
would-be robbers, finally chasing them off. Paul had yelled out,
"I hold for no one!" Too late, though, for Budd Philpot, who took
several fatal shots, and passenger Peter Roerig, who also died of
his wounds.[37]

Two posses were formed at once in Tombstone, one headed
by U. S. Deputy Marshal Virgil Earp, and the other by Cochise
County Sheriff Johnny Behan. Joining Virgil were Wyatt, Morgan,
Bat Masterson, and a few others, while Behan had his Deputy
Harry Woods and some cowboy hangers-on. The posses split up,
and Virgil's crew grabbed one of the fleeing bandits, Luther King.
Under "persuasion" by Morgan or Wyatt, Luther squealed and
claimed that he had only held the horses for Bill Leonard, Jim
Crane, and Harry Head. All of these fellows were peripheral
"cowboy" cronies, which explains some of the subsequent
happenings.[38]

Virgil turned over King to Sheriff Behan, who sent him back
to Tombstone with Deputy Sheriff Harry Woods. That was the last
seen of King. The prisoner "escaped" from Woods' custody, an
incident the Earps would recall as proving that Behan and his
crowd were in thick with the cowboy element. George Parsons
made the following comments in his diary:

King, the stage robber, escaped tonight early
from H. Woods who had been previously notified
of an attempt at release to be made. Some of our
officials should be hanged. They're a bad lot.[39]

Others could also make allegations. Doc Holliday had been a
close friend of Leonard in Las Vegas, New Mexico, and a few
witnesses claimed that Doc had been in on the planning of the
robbery; others stated that Doc had been seen riding hard earlier
in the day. The Earps, protecting Holliday, cried foul, saying that
this was just a diversion of Behan's crowd to shift the blame. On
the other hand, Fred Dodge, Wells, Fargo undercover man, always
believed that Doc had a role in the holdup.[40]

The posse work had been exhausting, as both posses were out
for days without food, and were thirty-six hours without water.
On the other hand, the fleeing robbers had been able to get fresh
mounts and were able to outdistance the posses headed by Virgil
Earp and Johnny Behan.[41]

No further arrests were made for the murders and the
attempted robbery. But the deaths, the work of Virgil's posse, and
the "leaky jail" provided by Behan aggravated the relations
between the two factions. By now the lines were clear-cut. Behan
was in constant company with the cowboys, burning to get
revenge on Wyatt, who had stolen his Sadie. Wyatt resented the
lucrative appointment Behan had received as Cochise County
Sheriff. Caution and distrust would now dominate all contact
between the two groups.

FOOTNOTES

1. Waters, *Earp Brothers*, p. 77.
2. At least one of the Earp brothers mining claims had been signed by December 9; copies of all of the Earp claims are in the Library, Arizona Historical Society, Tucson.
3. Lonnie E. Underhill, "The Tombstone Discovery: Recollections of Ed Schieffelin & Richard Gird," *Arizona and the West*, XXI (Spring, 1979), 37-75.
4. These comments on mining, and silver, are based on my research and writing on Western mining. The Tombstone ores are summarized in F. W. Galbraith, *Minerals of Arizona*, Bulletin 149, Arizona Bureau of Mines (Tucson, 1941). Two excellent contemporary accounts are by Wm. P. Blake, "Geology and Veins of Tombstone," *Transactions, American Institute of Mining Engineers*, X (1882), 334-39, and the July and October, 1880 issues of *Arizona Quarterly Illustrated*, which have company histories, biographies, and illustrations.
5. List of mining claims, in Library, Arizona Historical Society, Tucson.
6. Waters, *Earp Brothers*, p. 91.
7. Ibid., pp. 91-92.
8. Clum accounts abound. His papers are in the Special Collections, University of Arizona Library, Tucson. A typical Clum account is "It All Happened in Tombstone," *Arizona Historical Review*, II (October, 1929), 46-72.
9. The Parsons diaries for these years have been carefully transcribed and re-paged by Carl Chafin, and copies have been deposited in the Arizona Historical Society Library and in several other Western depositories.
10. Behan probably moved from Yavapai County to Pima

County in September or October of 1880.

11. It is hard to find a contemporary positive appraisal of Doc Holliday. Wyatt claims that once, in Dodge City, Doc saved his life, and from that time on, Wyatt became Doc's protector; Lake, *Wyatt Earp*, pp. 213-14.

12. Fred Dodge, *Undercover for Wells Fargo* (Boston, 1969), pp. 8-9.

13. Ibid., Appendix, contains several 1928 letters from Dodge to Stuart Lake, Wyatt's biographer.

14. For the lobbying for a new county, I used mostly the *Arizona Weekly Miner* of Prescott. The news out of the territorial capital was relevant, and many people from Prescott [in Yavapai County] had moved to the Tombstone area, so the *Miner* carried considerable news about the new mining district.

15. *Arizona Weekly Miner*, March 26, 1880.

16. Henry P. Walker, "Arizona Land Fraud: Model 1880; The Tombstone Townsite Company," *Arizona and the West*, XXI (Spring, 1979), 5-36. Walker's facts seem to be sound, but his interpretation is shaky. He claims that the land fraud problems caused the eventual shootout, etc. Some of the townsite controversy can be followed in the pages of the *Epitaph*, although Editor Clum, a vigorous opponent of Clark and Gray, is hardly objective.

17. Carl Chafin (ed.), *The West of George Whitwell Parsons*, entry for February 17, 1880, p. 157. All subsequent page references to the Parsons diaries are to the Chafin typescript volumes cited here; copies of these transcripts of the original diaries have been deposited in the Arizona Historical Society Library.

18. Wyatt's commission, and eventual resignation, are in the Recorder's Office, Pima County, Tucson.

19. Wm. Henry Bishop, "Across Arizona," *Harper's Monthly Magazine*, LXVI (March, 1883), 493-502.

20. The correspondence of Dake, Gosper, and other territorial officials is scattered with use of the word "cowboy" in its rustler-outlaw sense. The use of the word "cowboy" in any Western newspaper at this time implied "outlaw." For example, the Los Angeles *Times* of June 7, 1883, headlined an article "Cowboys in Inyo County," meaning robbers, desperadoes, etc.

21. Fremont address in Kelly, *Legislative History, Arizona*, pp. 98-99.

22. Stuart Lake to Ira Rich Kent of Houghton Mifflin Co., February 13, 1930, in Houghton Collection, Harvard University Library. This letter contained "poison" material Lake could not use in his biography of Wyatt, such as comments on the call girl past of Sadie Marcus, Wyatt's eventual wife.

23. Culled from many letters in the Stuart Lake Papers, Huntington Library, San Marino, California.

24. Alford E. Turner, *The O. K. Corral Inquest* (College Station, Texas, 1981), p. 156, from Wyatt Earp's testimony.

25. The Tucson *Arizona Weekly Citizen* of January 1, 1881, carried a full column on the Curly Bill proceedings, including verbatim testimony by Wyatt Earp. Parsons' diary, October 28, 1880, commenting on the death of Marshal White: "Bad state of things. Will be a bad winter I'm afraid."

26. See also Turner, *O.K. Corral Inquest*, pp. 30, 120, for Turner comments on the significance of the White incident.

27. Minutes, Tombstone Common Council, October 28, 1880;

these Minutes are in the Arizona Historical Society, Tucson, and have been carefully indexed by Carl Chafin.

28. Minutes, Tombstone Common Council, November 1, 1880.

29. Minutes, Tombstone Common Council, November 13, 1880 [election loss], November 15, 1880 [Virgil resigns].

30. Wyatt's resignation is in the Recorder's Office, Pima County, Tucson. The Tucson *Arizona Daily Star* of January 20, 1881, contained many details of the election fraud.

31. The Parson's diary entries for early January of 1881 contain some details of the election process, and his role in getting Clum elected.

32. Woods' role in creating the new county is mentioned in the *Arizona Weekly Miner* of January 21, 1881.

33. The seriousness of the differences between the Gosper and Fremont factions can be easily understood by reading the columns of the *Miner* during this period. See also Fireman, *American West*, Winter, 1964, for the Fremont-Gosper feud, and Jay W. Wagoner, *Arizona Territory, 1863-1912: A Political History* (Tucson, 1970), for Gosper's grabbing for the governorship.

34. The best testimony for the arrangement comes from Wyatt himself, when he went before Justice Wells Spicer during the shootout hearings; Turner, *O. K. Corral Inquest*, pp. 156-58. Wyatt seems arrogant and misled here, which gives greater credibility to his rendition.

35. The *Arizona Weekly Miner* of February 25, 1881, mocked Clum for crying over the appointment of Democrats to new positions in Cochise County.

36. The "Deuce" incident has a dozen interpretations, most of which can be followed in the contemporary press. One

interesting comment in Virgil's testimony later is that because he escorted the "Deuce" to jail in Tucson, he earned cowboy enmity; Turner, *O. K. Corral Inquest*, p. 196. Parsons' important diary entry on the "Deuce" affair is in Chafin (ed.), *Parsons*, January 14, 1881, p. 8. A decent account of the incident is by Lin Searles in "The Short Unhappy Life of Johnny-Behind-The-Deuce," *Frontier Times*, December-January, 1966, pp. 22-23, 44.

37. Newspapers in Tucson, Los Angeles, San Francisco, San Diego, etc., carried stories on the holdup and murders. See also Turner, *O. K. Corral Inquest*, pp. 167-68; Waters, *Earp Brothers*, p. 129; Dodge, *Undercover Agent*, p. 24; Parson's diary, March 16, 1881, p. 36; San Diego *Union*, April 14, 1881, on return of the posses.

38. An interesting summary of the capture and "disposition" of the King case is in Glenn Boyer (ed.), *I Married Wyatt Earp: The Recollections of Josephine Sarah Marcus Earp* (Tucson, 1976), pp. 33-36.

39. Chafin (ed.), *Parsons*, entry of March 28, 1881, pp. 41-42.

40. The question of Doc's participation has never been answered. I do not intend to investigate the possibilities here, although it should be pointed out that he was acquitted of these charges. The purpose of this work is to follow the doings of Virgil Earp, and there is not the slightest hint of funny business on his part in this affair.

41. Some details of the hardships suffered by the posse are in the "Tombstone" column of the San Diego *Union*, April 14, 1881.

IV: THE COWBOY MENACE

Events seemed to move at a more rapid pace for the Earps in late spring of 1881, in large part due to the lack of grit in City Marshal Ben Sippy. After the killing of Marshal Fred White in the Curly Bill episode, Virgil took over temporarily in the role of assistant city marshal, but Ben Sippy won the city marshal position in a special election. Then, in January of 1881, in the first election of the newly created city of Tombstone, Ben Sippy again beat out Virgil for the post.

Sippy must have needed the money, because he certainly didn't want and couldn't handle the position. He was a nice fellow who liked to gab with the guys in the saloons, but hated violence and confrontation. Allie referred to him as a coward. When Johnny-Behind-The-Deuce murdered engineer Philip Schneider, and there was a possibility of mob action by the miners in the streets of Tombstone to lynch the "Deuce," Sippy immediately called Virgil to give him a hand. Virgil was a deputy U. S. marshal, so this might have seemed like a reasonable request. It rankled

Virgil that Sippy, who had beat him out twice for the city marshal job, couldn't handle anything by himself.[1]

On the evening of June 6, when the city council was about to meet, one of the council members, seeing Wyatt in the street, stopped him, and the following conversation took place:

> Virgil, want to put you on as City Marshal, going to buy Ben Sippey off.
> Wrong man.
> Ain't you Virg?
> No, Wyatt.

This was not the first time the brothers were mistaken for one another, but Wyatt did not really know what was happening. In minutes it became very clear. Virgil was sent for, discussions were held:

> On motion, Chief of Police Sippy was granted two weeks leave of absence. . . .On motion, Virgil Earp was appointed Chief of Police, during absence of Sippy.[2]

Sippy was never seen again, at least not in Arizona Territory. One report had Sippy on an eastward-bound train, heading home to Pennsylvania. That is possible. Clum, the Earps, and a few other chroniclers didn't know what happened to Sippy, but they did feel the job was too tough for him, and the growing animosity between the cowboy faction and the town group [i.e., Earps] was something he wanted to avoid.

On June 22, in mid-afternoon, the first of Tombstone's fire disasters occurred. Several men in the Oriental saloon, while trying to determine the contents of a liquor barrel, did so with

POLICE DEPARTMENT.
CITY OF TOMBSTONE.

V. W. EARP,
CHIEF OF POLICE.

TOMBSTONE, A. T., *July 8 th* 188/

City of Tombstone

To George Bridge Dr.

to Seven days Work as Policeman

$7.00

V. W. Earp
Chief of Police

Virgil was the head of law enforcement in Tombstone, and the position was known both as Chief of Police and City Marshal. Arizona Historical Society

lighted cigars. There was an explosion, the alcohol quickly burned and spread the fire, and the Oriental and half of Tombstone's business district was soon engulfed in flames. Naturally, in this city that hadn't existed five years ago, the fire-fighting capabilities were limited.

Tombstone's wooden buildings went up in smoke like kindling wood. More than sixty structures were ablaze, from public buildings to saloons to grocery stores. Not much was spared in the eastern half of the business section. It was a wonder that the fire of Tombstone did not create dozens of tombstones. The only serious casualty was George Parsons, who while trying to fight the fire was caught on the second floor of a collapsing building. His head, especially his jaw and nose, was severely injured.[3]

Looters were not a problem in smoldering Tombstone. Because Tombstone was a new city, having shifted to its present location only two years earlier, and because this was a mining area, lot and claim jumping were continual problems. A fire, which confused everything and everyone, and threatened to wipe out known street boundaries, provided the ideal environment for lot jumpers. Furthermore, in the early stages, no one knew for certain how many people had been killed in the blaze. Clark and Gray, of the Tombstone Townsite Company, took advantage of the situation, hired some armed men, and had them put up tents on anything that resembled burned out or vacant land. If people were dead, who would protest if a lot jumper put up a tent on the dead man's site?

Virgil Earp would, and did. The mayor and the city council met with City Marshal Earp and told him to do anything he wanted in order to calm the situation and to prevent lot jumping. The first act of Marshal Earp was to stroll down the smoke-filled streets. He walked slowly, all six-feet-one of him, with pistol at his side, and Winchester cradled in his arms, carrying the double authority of a deputy U. S. marshal and a city marshal. He had to do a little buffaloing along the way, but the people on the streets of Tombstone knew what the official attitude towards lot-jumping was.

In his tours, Marshal Earp rounded up twenty-three men he could trust, swearing them in as special policemen to march the streets with him until morning, guaranteeing that all lots would be respected. Among these special policemen were his kid brother, Warren Earp, and Jack Vermillion, who would figure in later as a member of Wyatt's posses.

Fred Dodge, the Wells, Fargo undercover agent, was also one of the special policemen. Dodge later wrote that the main problem was on Allen and Sixth streets, where most of the houses of ill fame were situated. Many lot jumpers hired by Clark and Gray had put up tents and planned to sleep there during the night. Virgil's special policemen on horseback threw ropes over such tents and yelled, "Lot jumper, you *Git*!" And, reported Dodge, they did.[4]

Mayor John Clum as editor of the *Epitaph* reported what he felt about the new marshal:

> The unsettled title to lots led to some distur-
> bance between the lessees and lessors, but thanks
> to the prompt and decisive action of Marshal Earp
> there was no damage done. After consultation
> with the Mayor and Councilmen, and being told to
> use his own judgment in the matter, he appeared
> upon the scene of action and told the contestants
> that he should use his authority and the full power
> of the police force to maintain the same order of
> things that existed before the fire, and up to such
> time as the courts settle the question of titles. This
> decisive and just action on the part of the Marshal

John Clum, Mayor of Tombstone and editor of the Epitaph.
Arizona Quarterly Illustrated, January 1881

From Arizona Quarterly Illustrated, *July, 1880*

acted like oil upon troubled waters, and peace and order were restored. This action of Marshal Earp cannot be too highly praised, for in all probability it saved much bad blood and possibly bloodshed.[5]

Virgil received praise, as well as the steady income that went with the city marshal position. He also inherited young Warren Earp—restless, in his mid-twenties, and itching to be a man-about-town, but without the experience, frontier smarts, and level-headedness of older brothers James, Virgil, Morgan, and Wyatt. Warren had recently come to Tombstone from his parent's home in Colton, California, and was staying with Virgil and Allie. From time to time Virgil deputized Warren to help him earn a few dollars. He acted as a guard, collected a few taxes, and helped out with routine police chores. According to Allie, all Warren wanted was to "learn how to handle the pasteboards [faro cards] like Jim

97

and Morg and Wyatt, to be a marshal and wear a gun."[6]

On the evening of June 28, within days of the fire, the city council met and got right down to business. The office of chief of police was declared vacant, and "V. W. Earp was appointed Chief of Police. No dissenting votes." The council in particular wanted the chief of police to enforce the fire requirements, such as keeping excess rubbish off the streets, and "prevent the use of fire works within City limits on July fourth."

Times had changed. After Marshal White was killed, the city council—to their regret—called a special election, which was won by Ben Sippy. The council now realized that their man was at hand. There would be no special election. The job was vacant and was offered to Virgil W. Earp, who accepted the appointment. Although the official minutes usually referred to this position as "chief of police," the newspapers, and most locals, referred to the job as city marshal.

Some traditions would have us believe that Tombstone was a violent, shoot-em-up town, a place that "had a man for breakfast" every day. Enough documentation survives to put this myth to rest. Tombstone was on the edge of violence, as there were fights, shootings, and other raucous behavior in the saloons and on the streets. But once Sippy was out of the way, and Mayor Clum had given full encouragement to Marshal Earp, the situation calmed somewhat.

The power of the shoot-em-up myth is shown in the life and times of Wyatt Earp while he was a resident of Tombstone. He arrived in Tombstone in December of 1879 and left in the spring of 1882. In all that time he fired his pistol only once, during the famous shoot-out of October, 1881.

Virgil's salary as city marshal was $150.00 a month, and in addition he got a piece of the action on taxes collected, licenses issued, and fines levied. There was good money coming into the

Virgil Earp household now, and even Warren was earning a few dollars by being Virgil's deputy.[7]

When Virgil took over as city marshal, he made an inventory of materials on hand: two pair nippers [come-alongs, similar to handcuffs], one pair handcuffs, one water bucket, one tin cup, two slop buckets, and two pair blankets. There were five policemen on the staff, but changes occurred at once. One man—Tom Cornielson—was jailed for grand larceny, and another, A. Carrillo, resigned. Virgil had A. G. Bronk sworn in as policeman at once; he and Bronk had both served as nightwatchmen in Prescott a few years earlier.

There were forty-eight arrests made in Tombstone in the month of June, twenty-one of these for petty larceny. There were two assaults with a deadly weapons, two assaults and battery, three for carrying concealed weapons, and one for drawing a deadly weapon. Fourteen arrests were for fighting and disturbing the peace, primarily as a result of arguments that broke out in faro games. One man had been arrested for "fast-driving." Forty of those arrested had been slapped in jail; forty had been released. A total of $324.50 had been collected in fines, a healthy slice of which went into the pocket of the city marshal.

On July 4, Virgil took an official oath as chief of police of Tombstone, and included in the statement were a few more details of city property on hand related to law enforcement duties. He had six clubs, three belts, six stars, four whistles, five pairs of nippers, one pair of handcuffs, and one pair of leg irons.

The city marshal report for July listed sixty arrests, with the same types of violations prevailing: thirty-eight drunk and disorderly, nine fighting and disturbing the peace, two for carrying concealed weapons, one for discharging fire arms, one for fast riding, and so forth.

Tombstone in August must have been greatly slowed by the

heat, as there were only twenty-two arrests; the only unusual cases being three for "vulgar language." There was another arrest for fast riding; even Mayor Clum had once been arrested by Marshal Earp for going through the streets at break-neck speed. An interesting receipt in the auditor's records for August shows that Marshal Earp provided forty meals for prisoners, which came to a total of $10.00, all arranged from the nearby New York Bakery.

Virgil was so proud of the order that prevailed in Tombstone that on August 1 he presented the following statement to the city council:

> I am confident that the Same peace and quietness [sic] that exist now can be maintained with two Policemen and I would request that the Police force be reduced to two: and James Flynn and A. G. Bronk be kept on Police force.

Marshal Earp's request was honored, a fact that puzzles some historians. If Tombstone had been so wild a town, why didn't Marshal Earp realize its problems? Tombstone was not that wild, and Earp, as well as the city council, had proper measure of the situation.

The monthly report for September bears that out. There were only thirty-nine arrests, with nothing unusual; seventeen drunk and disorderly, nine for fighting and disturbing the peace, four for smoking opium, two for operating houses of ill fame, two for carrying concealed weapons, two for fast riding, and a few other minor crimes.

Virgil had pretty much quieted Tombstone, but he was not being over-confident. Both Flynn and Bronk were tough, reliable policemen, but Virgil knew many others in town that he could call on, either for posse work, or to quell any disturbance: Wyatt,

Tombstone Sept 27 – 188

SB Chapin
  City Auditor

        Sir

*I herewith return or License
No 592 with the following information
    (Emma Parker)*

*Refused payment party claims she
wants to make a Contested case*
            VW Earp
          License Collector

No 592   Class 14 $4 50

✦ CITY LICENSE. ✦

CITY AUDITOR'S OFFICE,

Tombstone, Cachise Co., A. T.,   SEP 28 1881   188

Received from *Emma Parker*
        Allen St.

the sum of *Four* _____ 50 Dollars, for License on the
business of *House of Ill Fame*

_____, Class *Two*, for the
term of *thirteen days* from *Sept 17* 1881
Edward B. Gage
    City Auditor.   EPITAPH PRINT   *John Carr*
                    Mayor.

*Licensing whorehouses was one of many duties for Virgil
Earp in Tombstone. In this particular case, a dispute arose. The
license was returned and no payment was made.* Arizona
Historical Society

Morgan, and Warren Earp, and Doc Holliday and Fred Dodge.

Another set of records that indicates the responsibility of the city marshal are the License Tax sheets for October. Virgil and his deputies collected more than $11,000.00 from the various business houses, which he deposited with the City Auditor.

A misunderstanding developed between Marshal Earp and Emma Parker, a madame who operated a house of ill fame. She had been licensed as a "Class Two" establishment, which operated in cycles of thirteen day licensing periods. On September 27, she refused to pay the fee, stating she intended to contest the case. Virgil filed a report on the matter. This is not mentioned here because it was a significant event. Rather, it adds to the picture of what constituted a month's work for a city marshal; collecting taxes, getting meals for prisoners, cleaning the hand cuffs, licensing whores, arresting drunks, and fining "fast riders."

The monthly reports, and a careful reading of the *Epitaph* and *Nugget* force the conclusion that Tombstone, at least during Marshal Virgil Earp's tour of duty, was not a boisterous, violent mining community. Most of the tough stuff took place in the saloons and gaming places, and those who entered such establishments knew the risks. The streets of Tombstone may have been dusty, but they were safe.

Tombstone may have been under control, but Cochise County was not. Although Virgil, as a deputy U. S. marshal, did have authority in Cochise County, his duties as city marshal kept him in Tombstone most of the time. Furthermore, Cochise County had a sheriff and deputies, who were supposedly enforcing the laws. They were not doing so, in part because of the size of Cochise County, in part because the county was newly established and therefore inexperienced in the ways of government, and in part because the sheriff was Johnny Behan, a friend, cohort, and partner of the very cowboys who were causing the problems.

During June and July of 1881, the border between Cochise County and the Mexican state of Sonora erupted in a series of actions, which included rustling, gun battles, intervention by the Mexican Army, and overall bitterness on both sides of the border. The cowboy faction was behind this, at one time murdering as many as fifteen Mexicans during a rustling raid.

A key event in this bloodshed happened on the morning of August 13. Newman Hayes [Old Man] Clanton, Jim Crane, and four other cowboys were caught with a herd of rustled cattle in Guadalupe Canyon, New Mexico, by Mexican soldiers. They were all wiped out in a revenge killing. Crane had been one of those accused in the holdup-murders of the Benson stage, and Old Man Clanton was one of the acknowledged leaders of the cowboy faction. With his passing, his son Ike became more prominent and would become the most outspoken opponent of the Earp Tombstone faction. A diary entry by George Parsons gives some feeling for the local attitudes about the incident:

> This killing business by the Mexicans, in my mind, was perfectly justifiable as it was in retaliation for killing of several of them and their robbery by cowboys recently, this same Crane being one of the number. Am glad they killed him. As for the others, if not guilty of cattle stealing, they had no business to be found in such bad company.[8]

The authorities were not oblivious to these border incidents but were handicapped by lack of funds and staff. For example, on May 30, 1881, U. S. Marshal Dake wrote to U. S. Attorney General Isaac W. MacVeagh in Washington:

> I am constantly in receipt of communications

103

complaining of the depredations of "cowboys" and other organized bands of outlaws who are operating in the southern part of this territory and raiding into Mexico, and asking the co-operation and assistance of the U. S. authorities in dispersing and bringing them to justice.[9]

Pretty much the same complaint was in a letter of June 23, from U. S. Attorney E. B. Pomroy in Tucson to MacVeagh:

Cowboys is a generic designation, originally applied to cow drivers and herders in Western Texas, but the name has been corrupted in the Territories of New Mexico and Arizona, and in its local significance includes the lawless element that exists upon the border, who subsist by rapine, plunder and highway robbery, and whose amusements are drunken orgies, and murder. . . .The crimes they commit, cattle stealing, highway robbing, assaults and murder, are cognizable by the Territorial authorities, and punishable by their laws; but owing to its magnitude the Territorial officers are unable to cope with the difficulty.[10]

Territorial Secretary Gosper received a lengthy letter from Joseph Bowyer of the Texas Consolidated Mining Company dated September 17, which included, in part:

The gang who are known as 'cowboys' are engaged in stock raiding in the valleys of San Simon and Cloverdale, in the South-eastern portion of Arizona, and from good authority I learn

John Gosper, a former roommate of Doc Holliday in Prescott, was Acting Governor and was friendly to the Clum-Earp faction. General John Fremont was governor of Arizona Territory during the Tombstone troubles, but spent most of his time out of the territory. Arizona Quarterly Illustrated, July, 1880

that the cattle, horses, and sheep, now controlled
by said cow-boys had been stolen from the citizens
of Sonora and Arizona and New Mexico. . . .The
cowboys frequently visit our town [Galeyville]
and often salute us with an indiscriminate discharge of firearms, and after indulging in a few
drinks at the saloons, practice shooting at the
lamps, bottles, glasses, etc., sometimes going to
the length of shooting the cigar out of ones
mouth.[11]

All of these communications, and newspaper coverage of
border incidents, shootings, and rustling, put considerable pressure on Secretary Gosper. He personally visited Tucson and
Tombstone, interviewed all principals, including the mayor,
sheriff, and city marshal, and wrote a report to Secretary of State
James G. Blaine.

Gosper stated that he needed money and men, but most of all
authority to act; after all, Fremont, the Governor, was never at
hand, so he was uncertain of his powers. Gosper reported that
Sheriff Behan could get no cooperation from Marshal Earp; "In
conversation with the Deputy U. S. Marshal, Mr. Earp, I found
precisely the same spirit of complaint existing against Mr. Behan
and his deputies."[12]

Gosper was appalled. In addition to this law enforcement
rivalry, Tombstone had two newspapers, which had also taken
sides. The U. S. Army, with several nearby posts, was prohibited
by law from getting involved in civilian law enforcement situations.

What Gosper did not report, but which he undoubtedly knew,
was that personal factors had also influenced the bitterness. Sheriff
Behan had never appointed Wyatt Earp his deputy, as had been the

THE SHERIFF OF TOMBSTONE AND HIS CONSTITUENTS.

Bishop, who wrote the Tombstone article for Harper's, *referred to the "The Sheriff of Tombstone." Actually, it was Johnny Behan, sheriff of the newly created Cochise County, with Tombstone as county seat.* Harper's Monthly, March, 1883

arrangement. Furthermore, Wyatt had stolen Behan's live-in girl friend, Sadie Marcus, and they had set up housekeeping in Tombstone.

Another element that added to the growing enmity in the two camps was a move by Wyatt to infiltrate the cowboys, make an arrest coup, and get great newspaper coverage; this, he felt, would aid his cause in 1882 when he intended to run against Johnny Behan for sheriff of Cochise County. In Wyatt's own words:

> I had an ambition to be Sheriff of this County
> at the next election, and I thought it would be a
> great help to me with the people and businessmen
> if I could capture the men who killed Philpot.[13]

Wyatt approached Ike Clanton, Frank McLaury, and Joe Hill with a deal. They could have the reward money, if Wyatt got the glory. All they would have to do would be to turn over or reveal the location of Leonard, Head, and Crane, who were wanted for the murders. Wyatt got Wells, Fargo to increase the reward money.

A deal was struck, but quickly went haywire. Head and Leonard were killed in New Mexico, and Crane was wiped out with Clanton's father in the border incident. Then fear, anger, and bitterness set in, as Clanton, McLaury, and Hill worried that word would leak out that they had arranged to snitch on the trio. They also accused Wyatt and Virgil of telling Doc Holliday, and perhaps others, of the arrangement. Such news, if it did leak out, would do Clanton and gang no good in Cochise County. This bitterness was one additional, powerful factor in bringing out the Earp-cowboy confrontation.

Another series of incidents involving yet another stage robbery gave further reasons for the cowboy faction to hate the Earps.

Johnny Behan, sheriff of the newly created Cochise County.
Arizona Historical Society

On September 8, at ten p.m. near Bisbee, three or four masked men held up the stage, rifled the Wells, Fargo treasure box, robbed a few passengers of cash and watches, and stole the U. S. Mail. The next morning, two posses were formed in Tombstone. One was headed by County Sheriff Johnny Behan, and the other by Deputy U.S. Marshal Virgil Earp. The theft of the U. S. Mails was enough to account for Virgil's presence. He deputized Wyatt, Morgan, and others in the Earp camp to be part of his posse.

In Bisbee, it was learned that Frank Stilwell, ex-deputy sheriff under Behan, had had heels replaced in his boots. This fit the clue that had been discovered—unusual footprints had been found at the scene of the robbery. In later years both Bill Breakenridge and Wyatt Earp would claim to have found this information. Breakenridge also claimed that it was obvious that Stilwell was the robber; witnesses had reported one of the masked men using phrases that were peculiar to Stilwell, such as "sugar" for money.

Marshal Earp arrested Stilwell and Pete Spence for stage robbery, and took them before Justice Wells Spicer in Tombstone. Stilwell was released on bail; Virgil promptly arrested him again, this time on charges of stealing the U. S. Mails, and delivered him to Tucson. Stilwell was acquitted of all charges on October 20, but he had built up enough bitterness against the Earps to involve him in deadly conspiracies.[14]

On October 4, word reached Tombstone of a fight between the U. S. Army and unidentified Indians in the Dragoon Mountains, twenty miles northeast of Tombstone. Word spread rapidly through town, and near-panic set in; Parsons, who like everyone else was alarmed, referred to it as the "Indian scare." The San Diego *Union* of October 6 reported:

> Mayor Clum and Chief of Police Earp are now
> raising a company of men to go out and intercept

110

the Indians if they go south. They have sent
messengers to the mining companies to get arms,
they all having a large number of rifles and
ammunition.

George Parsons borrowed a Winchester and joined the party
of forty armed men, which he stated was headed by Mayor Clum,
Sheriff Behan, and City Marshal Earp. Parsons reported:

On the outskirts chose Sheriff Behan, Captain,
and Earp, First Lieutenant. We then called off by
fours, every fourth man to hold horses in engage-
ment, and quickly went for the trail.[15]

The posse was next to a fiasco, as they couldn't locate the
Indians, and a "terrible rainstorm" set in, soaking everyone,
getting clothes, food, and guns wet and muddy. Some in the posse
"slunk away," and Mayor Clum and Parsons couldn't keep up
with the party, as the muddy soil caused their horses to go in
"nearly up to their knees at times." On October 8, the San Diego
Union gave an up-date on the affair, provided by Major Thomas
Sorin, one of the founders of the *Epitaph* and a member of the
posse. The Indians were headed for the border, and aside from
stealing a few horses, they had not caused any great outbreak of
violence.

On this posse, like several others in which both Virgil Earp and
Johnny Behan participated, the posse split in two, each man
leading a portion. Behan was in charge, most likely because he was
the sheriff, and this was in rural Cochise County. No chroniclers
seem to have asked why it was that City Marshal Virgil Earp
participated in such actions outside of the city limits. A more
reasonable approach would have been to question the presence of

111

Mayor Clum on such a posse; perhaps he was there as a reporter for his newspaper, the *Epitaph*. Virgil's presence can be explained on several grounds: he was fearless, he was a crack shot, he had considerable experience, and although he was city marshal, he was also a deputy U. S. marshal with a direct link to Marshal Dake in the territorial capital in Prescott.

FOOTNOTES

1. Waters, *Earp Brothers*, p. 115.
2. This conversation is constructed from the Lake-Wyatt Earp interview notes, Lake Papers, Huntington Library. The last line reads: "Sent Virg in, talked, bt. Sippey off. Virg got job." The motion is from the Minutes, Tombstone Common Council, June 6, 1881.
3. There was continual coverage of the fire and aftermath in much of the Western press; see, for example, the details in the San Diego *Union* of June 23, 1881. Parsons had some interesting comments in his diary, but only after he recovered from his injuries.
4. Dodge, *Undercover*, pp. 34-35.
5. *Epitaph*, June 23, 1881.
6. Waters, *Earp Brothers*, pp. 112-13, 117.
7. The detailed information which follows is drawn from several dozen documents in the Medigovitch Collection, Arizona Historical Society, Tucson. These documents include personnel rosters, equipment lists, salaries, arrests, and so forth.
8. Chafin (ed.), *Parsons*, entry of August 17, 1881, p. 101.
9. This letter, and the few that are mentioned below, are in the Special Collections, University of Arizona Library, Tucson, and in the U. S. Marshal's Office, McLean, Virginia.
10. Pomroy letter of June 23, 1881.
11. Bowyer letter of September 17, 1881.
12. Gosper to Blaine, August 18, 1881.
13. Turner, *O. K. Corral Inquest*, p. 156.

14. For the Bisbee stage incident, see Lake, *Wyatt Earp*, pp. 274-75; Breakenridge, *Helldorado*, Chapter XI; San Diego *Union*, March 25, 1882, obituary of Stilwell.
15. Chafin (ed.), *Parsons*, p. 126.

V: SHOOTOUT IN TOMBSTONE

With the passing of time, history has pretty much determined that Wyatt Earp was the leading character in the famous Tombstone gunfight, usually referred to as the Shootout at the O.K. Corral. There is little in the contemporary record to back up such an elevated role for Wyatt. Virgil was the man in charge. However, subsequent events which put Virgil out of action, and by which Wyatt got involved in the most famous vendetta in the West, influenced how historians and the general public have viewed this famous shootout.

There were many reasons why the Earps and the cowboy faction were at odds. Some of these have been detailed earlier, and other relevant points were baldly stated by leading observers and participants in the Justice Wells Spicer hearings which followed the shootout. What finally triggered the confrontation were the strong feelings between Ike Clanton and Doc Holliday.

At noon on October 25, Ike Clanton and Tom McLaury rode into town in a wagon. McLaury was carrying thousands of dollars,

115

Joseph "Ike" Clanton, who probably triggered the animosity that led to the Tombstone shootout, was not a casualty there. Ike was killed by a sheriff's posse in Graham County, Arizona, in 1887. New-York Historical Society

Tom McLaury. Arizona Historical Society

117

meant to pay a debt to butcher James Kehoe; cowboy opponents would point to this as merely another payoff relating to rustled beef. Ike and Tom also wanted to do some drinking and gambling, and Ike was looking for a showdown with Doc Holliday.

Ike and Tom boozed and gambled for hours, and around one a.m. on October 26, in the Alhambra Saloon, Ike and Doc started yelling at each other. Ike accused Doc of spilling the beans about the agreement worked out between Wyatt and Ike to capture the robbers of the Benson stage. Clanton wasn't armed, so Doc, denying Ike's claims, yelled at him:

Go heel yourself!

Morgan Earp was on hand, and he pushed Doc outside the saloon before anything serious erupted. Ike followed, and there was a hot exchange of words among Ike, Morgan, and Doc.

At this juncture, City Marshal Virgil Earp appeared, was informed about the argument, and threatened both Doc and Ike with jail unless they knocked it off. Wyatt Earp then came by and hustled off the still fuming Doc Holliday, taking him to his rooms at Fly's Boarding House near the O. K. Corral. Ike, seeing he was in no danger now, stated that they [the cowboys] would be "after you all in the morning."[1]

What followed next is a bit puzzling, but all sides agree on the matter. Ike went to the Occidental and got in an all-night poker game with Tom McLaury, Marshal Virgil Earp, Sheriff Johnny Behan, and a few others, indeed a weird array of men around a gambling table. Throughout the early morning hours, Ike kept grumbling, making threats against Holliday, and even included Holliday's buddies—the Earps—in his condemnations. This implied that Ike Clanton was either a bold man, or a dumb one. Several witnesses claimed that during the all-night poker game,

John H. "Doc" Holliday. Arizona Historical Society

Wyatt Earp. Arizona Historical Society

Morgan Earp. Arizona Historical Society

121

Marshal Earp had his pistol resting on his lap.

The game broke up about dawn, and the principals began to scatter. Outside the saloon, Ike stopped Virgil and asked him to carry a message to Holliday:

> I asked him what it was. He said, "The damned son of a bitch has got to fight." I said, "Ike, I am an officer and I don't want to hear you talking that way at all. I am going down home now, to go to bed, I don't want you to raise any disturbance while I am in bed."[2]

Off and on during the next few hours, several witnesses saw Ike Clanton wandering through the streets of Tombstone, threatening Holliday and the Earps, pistol by his side, and a Winchester cradled in his arms. This, of course, was in violation of the city ordinance prohibiting the carrying of firearms while in the city. Ike's blustering must have been fueled on alcohol, but he was not entirely out of his mind. He knew precisely where the Earps and Holliday were—home in bed—but contented himself with posturing in the streets of Tombstone. A few friends went to the homes of Virgil and Wyatt, including Policman A. G. Bronk, but neither Virgil nor Wyatt bothered to get out of bed; Ike was a notorious loud-mouth, and the Earp brothers assumed that he would soon be snoring the sleep of a tired drunk.

In late morning, Mayor Clum, just leaving the *Epitaph* office on his way to lunch in the Grand Hotel, spotted Ike at the southeast corner of Fourth and Fremont, with a Winchester in hand talking to a cowboy:

> Hello Ike! Any new war?

Clum was baiting Ike a little, but on the other hand, if there was a story in this for the *Epitaph*, why not get it? Clum later wrote:

> The remarkable feature of the situation was that Ike actually was out on the war-path and was at that very moment seeking an opportunity to pot our valiant Chief of Police, and although I was mayor of the city, no hint of this serious situation had yet reached me.[3]

By now, Marshal Earp had heard that not only was Ike still fulminating, but he was doing so with a Winchester. Virgil got out of bed, went around to get Wyatt, and while walking down the street they met Morgan. Almost at that exact moment, Wyatt and Virgil spotted Ike, right after Clum had saluted him with the "war cry." The Earps approached Ike, and while Wyatt diverted Ike's attention, Marshal Earp grabbed Ike's Winchester. Ike reached for his pistol, which he was carrying in his belt, but Marshal Earp buffaloed him across the skull. Virgil's testimony:

> I hit him over the head with mine [pistol] and knocked him to his knees and took his six-shooter from him. I ask him if he was hunting for me. He said he was, and if he had seen me a second sooner he would have killed me. I arrested Ike for carrying firearms, I believe was the charge, inside the city limits.[4]

Virgil was referring to City Ordinance #9, Section 1, which stated that it was illegal to carry "deadly weapons, concealed or otherwise, within the limits of the City of Tombstone."

Marshal Earp and Wyatt had used deception in disarming Ike, diverting his attention, grabbing his Winchester, then buffaloing him. There is only one reasonable way to consider that event: the Earps, officers of the law, knew how to defuse a blustering, threatening, armed drunk.

The bleeding Ike Clanton was hauled off to the chambers of Judge Albert O. Wallace. While Virgil went to find the judge, Wyatt, Morgan, and Ike engaged in a torrid verbal exchange in the judge's chambers, with charges of thief, liar, and other epithets bouncing off the walls. Ike bragged that he would soon get all the Earps, so Morgan gave him a chance by offering Ike a six-shooter; Ike declined.

Judge Wallace and Marshal Earp arrived, and Ike was fined $25.00 for carrying firearms. Marshal Earp then took Ike's pistol and Winchester to the Grand Hotel; Ike could pick them up on his way out of town.[5]

When Wyatt left Judge Wallace, one of the first people he ran into was Tom McLaury. Wyatt, bitter now, and having just come from an encounter with McLaury's mentor Ike Clanton, demanded of McLaury: was he heeled, that is, carrying a gun?

Witnesses did not agree on the response, but Wyatt claimed that Tom McLaury was carrying a gun inside his pants on his right hip. McLaury gave a gruff reply, so Wyatt punched him in the face and buffaloed him over the head, leaving McLaury dazed and collapsed on the street. Wyatt was acting as an officer of the law; Marshal Earp had deputized him to help handle the Ike Clanton affair. Yet, Wyatt's action had been brutal and intimidating. If McLaury had indeed been carrying a weapon, he should have been arrested.[6]

Around this same time, Billy Clanton and Robert [Frank] McLaury arrived in town on horseback; both had Winchesters in their saddle scabbards and were carrying pistols in their holsters.

Frank McLaury. Arizona Historical Society

In spite of some claims that Ike Clanton had telegrammed Billy and Frank to come in from nearby Charleston, it seemed that the two actually were coming to town on business, to help Tom McLaury straighten out his debt with butcher Kehoe [at Bauer's Market].

As the two rode up to the Grand Hotel, Doc Holliday stepped out into the street and shook Billy Clanton's hand in greeting. There is no reasonable explanation for Doc's unusual handshake. He and the Clantons were only slightly acquainted with each other; in fact, Doc and the cowboy crowd had little in common.[7]

Billy and Frank went into the Grand for a drink, and there they learned that Ike Clanton and Tom McLaury had both been buffaloed in the recent hours. Minutes later, all four principals of the cowboy faction gathered in Spangenberg's gun shop—Ike Clanton, Tom McLaury, Billy Clanton, and Frank McLaury.

While Billy and Frank were stuffing cartridges into their gunbelts, Wyatt Earp walked by the front of Spangenberg's, saw what was going on inside, and noticed Frank McLaury's horse on the sidewalk. Odds of four to one did not faze Wyatt Earp. He backed Frank's horse off the sidewalk, as a city ordinance prohibited such practice. The cowboys came out of the gun shop, and Frank argued with Wyatt, but the result was the same. The horse remained off the sidewalk.

During this exchange of hot words, Marshal Virgil Earp walked up, but didn't say anything—his deputy seemed to have the situation well in hand.[8]

One puzzling aspect of the above confrontation is that neither Marshal Virgil Earp nor his Deputy Wyatt arrested the cowboys for carrying firearms. It was obvious by now that Virgil and Wyatt had no fear of the cowboys. It may have been that in the heated exchange it was revealed that the cowboys were about to leave town. If so, they were entitled to have their firearms with them.

The sidewalk incident resulted in one further humiliation of the cowboys by the Earp faction. Many residents had witnessed the buffaloing of Ike Clanton and Frank McLaury, and now more Tombstone folk saw Wyatt alone force four cowboys to cower. Ike may have been a borderline coward, but the other three did not share that reputation. They would have to do something to recover respect, or could never show their faces again in Tombstone.

By now the town was abuzz, residents scurrying around telling each other about the day's encounters, and predicting more trouble ahead. A citizens' committee had formed and talked with Marshal Earp for a few minutes. Some members asked Virgil to disarm the cowboys before violence erupted. Virgil decided to let the cowboys have their "mouth," and leave town. By this time the four cowboys had gone from Dunbar's stable towards the O. K. Corral. Virgil stated that if they remained in the Corral, he would consider the day's excitement over. If they came out on the street, "I would take their arms off and arrest them."[9]

The news had also spread to the cowboy faction, and the four were joined by Billy "The Kid" Claiborne, Wesley Fuller, and Billy Allen. The cowboy party walked down through an alley via the O. K. Corral, into Fremont Street, turned left and were holed up in a small lot, between William Harwood's house and Fly's boarding house; Fly's photo studio was directly behind the boarding house.

The Justice Spicer hearings contain many opinions as to what happened next, and who started what move. However, one witness who deserves more attention than most is H. F. Sills, a Nevada railroad engineer new in town. He was by Harwood's lot, saw the cowboys, and overheard considerable cursing and threats. Part of his testimony:

I saw four or five men standing in front of the

127

O. K. Corral, talking of some trouble they had with Virgil Earp, and they made threats at the time, that on meeting him they would kill him on sight. Someone of the party spoke up at the time and said that they would kill the whole party of the Earps when they met them. I then walked up the street and made enquiries to know who Virgil Earp and the Earps were. A man on the street pointed out Virgil Earp to me and told me that he was the city marshal. I went over and called him to one side and told him the threats I had overheard this party make. One of the men had a bandage around his head at the time, and the day of the funeral he was pointed out to me as Isaac Clanton. I recognized him as one of the party.[10]

The situation being what it was, coupled with the warning from bystanders such as Sills, Virgil Earp determined that he would have to act in the matter. He was the city marshal, and in addition was a deputy U. S. marshal. Law and order would suffer in image, if not reality, if the cowboys were not immediately disarmed. With Marshal Earp were three men whom he deputized to help him handle the cowboys—Wyatt Earp, Morgan Earp, and Doc Holliday. The four officers of the law left the area in front of Hafford's Saloon on the northeast corner of Fourth and Allen, walked north on Fourth, then turned left on Fremont Street and headed towards Harwood's lot. Each was armed with a six-shooter. In addition, Virgil carried a double-barreled shotgun which he had taken from the Wells, Fargo stock.

As the four advanced, they made some shifts in armaments. None of the four were wearing holsters; all carried their pistols in their hands, belts, or in their pockets. Doc Holliday was the only

Virgil Earp. Arizona Historical Society

one wearing a long coat, so Virgil gave Doc the sawed-off shotgun to put under the coat, in order not to alarm the citizens. In exchange, Doc passed his cane to Virgil, who carried it in his left hand.[11]

Some other heads and hands also tried to stop any confrontation and had sent for Sheriff Behan, who was getting shaved at Barron's Barber Shop. Behan went to Hafford's corner and asked Marshal Earp about the excitement. Virgil said there were "a lot of sons-of-bitches in town looking for a fight." Behan later testified that he had urged Virgil to disarm the cowboys, but that Virgil preferred instead to have them fight. The Earp testimony was that anything Behan stated was bound to be suspect.

Sheriff Behan volunteered to disarm the cowboys. He went to them, and what followed was learned from the intriguing testimony of several witnesses. Behan asked them to disarm; he told them to disarm; he begged them to disarm. In his own words:

> Boys, you must give up your arms. . . .You
> have got to give up your arms. . . .Boys, you must
> go up to the Sheriff's Office and lay off your arms,
> and stay there until I get back. . . .I told them I was
> going to disarm the other party.[12]

Sheriff Behan glanced up Fremont Street and saw the four in the Earp party advancing. He said to the Clanton group, "wait here. I see them coming down. I will go up and stop them."

As the Earps advanced, Sheriff Behan met them by Bauer's Market and told them to go no further, and stated that he intended to disarm the Clanton gang. "Gentleman, I am Sheriff of this County, and I am not going to allow any trouble if I can help it." Behan's testimony is used here because although it is anti-Earp in intent, it shows how ineffectual Behan was as a lawman. Also, he

Doc Holliday's name has become synonymous with "shot-gun." The gun was Virgil's, taken from a rack in the police chief's office. Ben Carlton Mead illustration, True West, February 1960

was paying the price for being too friendly with the cowboy-rustler faction. It seemed that everyone was ignoring Sheriff Behan. To continue with Behan's testimony:

> They brushed past me. I turned and went with
> them. I was probably a step or two in the rear as
> we went down the street. I was expostulating with
> them all this time.

The final pre-shootout scene, then, consists of Marshal Virgil Earp with his three deputies going to disarm and arrest the cowboys, with a bleating, pleading sheriff trailing behind.

Virgil Earp was disgusted with Behan's weaknesses, and with his constant protection of the cowboy crew. Virgil was the city marshal of Tombstone, and he would make the law enforcement decisions in this town. Virgil and Wyatt, who had spent the morning conking the cowboys on the skull, were intent on ending the troubles. Behan, although sheriff, had no more courage or expertise now than he had had in Prescott in 1879 when he got beaten up in a Chinese laundry and couldn't get his pistol to work.

Among the cowboys, the Clanton friends had begun to scatter; Wes Fuller and Billy Allen, although armed, started to backtrack, and Billy Claiborne was thinking along the same lines. Ike Clanton was not armed; Marshal Earp had placed Ike's guns in the Grand Hotel. Frank McLaury and Billy Clanton were wearing holstered Colts, and each had a rifle in a saddle scabbard. Tom McLaury had checked his pistol at Mehan's Capitol Saloon when he arrived in town; some witnesses, though, maintained that Tom was still armed.[13]

Therefore, the four in the Earp party were armed with four pistols and one shotgun. In the Clanton party, Ike was unarmed,

132

Sketch of shootout. Turner, The Earps Talk

133

Billy Clanton and Frank McLaury had holstered pistols, and Tom McLaury was most likely unarmed.

As the Earps neared Harwood's lot, Virgil shifted the cane from his left hand to his gun hand, figuring that this would be an indication that violence was not planned. As they reached the lot, Virgil was on the left, to his right was Wyatt, then Doc, and on the outside, Morgan.

Frank McLaury stood against the side of Harwood's house, holding the reins to his horse. To Frank's right were Billy Clanton and horse, then Tom McLaury. Billy Claiborne was farther back in the lot, and Ike stood closest to the advancing Earps at the edge of the street, at the corner of Fly's rooming house.

Marshal Virgil Earp yelled at the cowboys, "Throw up your hands!" At once, Billy Clanton and Frank McLaury moved their hands towards their holstered pistols, and Tom McLaury jumped behind Frank's horse. Virgil shouted:

Hold on, I don't want that!

The words are not controversial, but their objective is. Many students of the shootout now believe that Virgil was directing his words to the rest of the Earp party, who were itching to fight the cowboys.[14]

Shots erupted in a thirty-second gunfight that has defined all gunfights since. Little is known about who shot at whom, who hit whom, or any of the other details cluttered into this half-minute encounter.

There is not even agreement as to who shot first. If only two of the cowboys were armed, it seems unlikely that one of them would have started a pistol duel. On the other hand, with Virgil's words, Billy Clanton and Frank McLaury dropped their hands to their pistols, so it is possible that they drew and fired first.

In the Earp party, it is incontrovertible that Marshal Virgil Earp not only did not want a gun fight, he also carried a cane in his gun hand. Furthermore, he was the most prudent of the four, and was carrying the full force of the law. Wyatt—cold, steely-eyed Wyatt—was bitter about the cowboys and about Behan and could have shot first; in the coming years he would gladly take credit for firing the first shot. Doc Holliday, gambler, veteran of many a scrape, and dying of tuberculosis, always walked the thin line and could easily have forced the fight. Morgan, a pleasant fellow, good company, also had a violent temper and could easily have pulled the trigger first.

As soon as the shooting commenced, Ike Clanton ran up and grabbed Wyatt's left arm. Wyatt testified:

> I could see no weapon in his hand, and thought
> at the time he had none, and so I said to him, "The
> fight has commenced. Go to fighting or get away,"
> at the same time pushing him off with my left hand,
> like this. He started and ran down the side of the
> building.[15]

This situation, described also by others, puts the lie to Ike's claim later that the entire shootout was an attempt by the Earp party to assassinate him.

Although a vicious shootout occurred, there will be no attempt here to recreate it. Many others have done so, yet no account is satisfactory. Some of the leading participants were killed, others [such as Ike] had only a partial view of the unfolding event, and the others—the Earp faction—had points of view carefully honed by the best frontier lawyers. The only recourse for the avid student of the affair is to read the accounts in the *Epitaph* and *Nugget*, along with the testimony from the Justice Spicer hearings.

Of the many shots exchanged, a few were verified by several witnesses. One of Wyatt's shots hit Billy Clanton's horse, which bolted. Doc blasted Tom McLaury with two barrels of the shotgun. Virgil took a hit in the leg, probably from Billy Clanton, and Morgan got a bullet in the shoulder. As he fell, Morgan put a shot into Frank McLaury's head, just as McLaury's last shot hit Doc Holliday in his hip holster. Virgil then blasted Billy Clanton again.

Billy Clanton and Frank McLaury fired their last shots while on the ground; Billy, shot through the right wrist, was using his left hand to fire, asking anyone for more cartridges. This was the end of the pathetic display. Photographer C. S. Fly, with a Henry Rifle in his arms, walked cautiously up from nearby and lifted the empty six-gun from Billy Clanton's hands. Tom McLaury died almost instantly; Frank McLaury died shortly after the fighting stopped; and Billy Clanton died within the hour. Of the four in the cowboy gang, only Ike Clanton escaped, luckily being pushed away by Wyatt Earp, who could have easily killed him.

Among the Earps, Virgil had taken a shot in the leg, Morgan was wounded in the shoulder, and Doc had a wound on his hip where he wore his holster. Wyatt Earp came out of the battle unscathed. The *Epitaph* account next day included these words:

> Wyatt Earp stood up and fired in rapid succession, as cool as a cucumber, and was not hit . . .
> Doc Holliday was as calm as though at target practice and fired rapidly.

The funeral, which took place on October 27, was one of the major events in Tombstone history, with hundreds of people on hand to follow the local brass band down Allen Street to the cemetery. Clum's *Epitaph* gave a detailed account of the ceremony, concluding that "it was a most impressive and saddening sight and such a one as it is to be hoped may never occur again in this community." The funeral, though, began a shift in community feeling toward the Earps. The cry of "murder" began to be heard, especially through the columns of the *Nugget*.

A coroner's jury met and came to the unastounding conclusion that the McLaury boys and Billy Clanton had come to their deaths "from the effects of pistol and gunshot wounds inflicted by Virgil Earp, Morgan Earp, Wyatt Earp, and one Holliday commonly called 'Doc' Holliday."

Mayor Clum, for all his posturing in later years as a champion of the Earps, bowed to public pressure. The city council met on October 29—the same day that Ike Clanton filed murder charges against the Earps. The council minutes read:

> Mayor Clum stated that meeting was called to consider grave charges against Chief of Police Earp and it was ordered that pending investigation of said charges Chief Earp be temporarily suspended and James Flynn act as Chief during such suspension.

An arrest warrant was made out, and Virgil, Morgan, Wyatt and Doc Holliday were arrested by Sheriff Behan. Because they were confined to bed, Morgan and Virgil were not served, so only Wyatt and Doc Holliday were taken into custody.

Hearings were held, beginning on October 31, which lasted through November, before Justice of the Peace Wells Spicer. Although Spicer as a justice could not rule in such capital crimes as murder, he did have the authority to determine whether there was cause for the case to go before a higher court. Spicer, in

137

addition to being a justice, was also a mining attorney and wrote mining columns for the Tucson *Star*. It is generally conceded that Spicer favored the Earp faction. He, Mayor Clum, Marshal Earp, and the leading mining figures in the community were generally of like mind. For example, when bail money was needed by the Earps, local mining moguls E. B. Gage and James Vizina were quick to participate.

It might be well at this point to consider why community support had started to drift from the Earps. Although Tombstone was a mining community and the cowboys were considered "outsiders," there were lots of cowboys and their backers in the environs of Tombstone, and they filled the community for days after the shootout, crying foul and claiming that the dead trio were unarmed, or that they had been killed in a vicious manner by the plotting Earps. Vigorous reporting in the *Nugget* buttressed their point of view.

Meanwhile, spreading his share of vitriol throughout the county was Sheriff Johnny Behan, who as usual had demonstrated on the day of the shooting that he couldn't handle conflict. Behan was in his glory now, befriending even further the cowboy crowd, talking against the Earps, and getting revenge for the many humiliations suffered at their hands. The whole community also knew of Behan's ex-girl friend Sadie, now living with Wyatt. Here Behan had a chance to give his all towards getting revenge. Conviction of the Earps would help tip the scales in his favor.

The hearings, like the shootout, cannot be summarized with much degree of clarity. Forty witnesses testified during the month, including Ike Clanton, the Earps, Behan, Billy Claiborne, Wes Fuller, H. F. Sills, and Billy Allen. Also testifying were witnesses who saw a portion of the event, or overheard remarks. The testimony appeared in almost complete accounts in the

Nugget and the *Epitaph*, and in recent years has been made available in Alford E. Turner's *The O. K. Corral Inquest*.

The Earps' defense team was headed by Tom Fitch, the "silver-tongued orator," the politician from Nevada and Arizona Territory, member of the territorial legislature, and at the time practicing law out of Tucson. The Clanton-McLaury interests were handled by Lyttleton Price, the district attorney, and Attorneys Benjamin Goodrich and J. S. Robinson. The Clanton-McLaury cause was helped with the addition of an attorney from Fort Worth, Will McLaury, brother to Frank and Tom. McLaury was convinced that his brothers had been murdered, and he volunteered his help toward convicting the Earps.

In the month-long hearings, Attorney Fitch never called on Morgan Earp or Doc Holliday to present evidence, most likely fearing that their tempers and attitudes would not make them good witnesses. Justice Spicer also permitted Wyatt to read into the record a lengthy statement, most likely prepared by Fitch. He was not cross-examined on the substance of his statement.

Marshal Virgil Earp testified on November 19 and was cross-examined on November 22. Virgil provided much detail on the problem with the Clantons and with Sheriff Behan's failure to disarm them. He also claimed that Behan had told him, "I have disarmed them all." According to Virgil, it was this statement by Behan that led him to shift the cane to his right hand, to indicate to the cowboys that he had peaceful intentions.

Virgil also explained what legal authority Wyatt, Morgan, and Doc had at the time of the shootout—he had deputized them. One of his responses began with these words:

> When I called Morgan Earp, Wyatt Earp, and
> Doc Holliday to go and help me disarm the
> McLaurys and Clantons. . . .[16]

139

Another interesting detail provided by Marshal Earp concerned his own activities during the shootout:

> (Q) How many shots did you fire, and at whom?
> (A) I fired four shots. One at Frank McLaury, and I believe the other three were at Billy Clanton. I am pretty positive one was at Frank McLaury and three at Billy Clanton.

The judgement of Wells Spicer in Territory of Arizona vs. Morgan Earp, et al Defendants, is fascinating reading, not only because of the shootout information, but because of its consideration of the handling of frontier law and order. Spicer understood the many varying points of view, knew of the divided sentiments in the community, and was aware of the hostility between the city marshal faction and that of the sheriff.

Spicer's words deserve to be read in their entirety, but only a few salient points will be mentioned here. Most importantly, he concluded that there was no evidence that the case against the Earps deserved to go to trial. "I order them to be released."

The justice demolished Ike Clanton's claim of "assassination," and also pointed out that Behan himself had admitted that the cowboys were armed, and that he had been unable to disarm them. Whether or not some or all of the cowboys were armed was not relevant:

> The defendants were officers charged with the duty of arresting and disarming armed and determined men who were expert in the use of firearms, as quick as thought and as certain as death and who had previously declared their intention not to be

140

Justice Spicer. Arizona Historical Society

arrested nor disarmed. Under the statutes, as well
as the common law, they have a right to repel force
with force.

So far as the affair being "murder," Spicer pointed out that
witnesses on both sides stated that the three deceased men had
kept shooting to the last, with "unflinching bravery"; this did not
seem to Justice Spicer to be the act of unwilling victims being
slaughtered.

Spicer included many of the points of disagreement in his
decision, but continually stressed that the cowboy element
represented violence and illegality. The following are Spicer's
most telling words in the decision:

> In view of the past history of the county and
> the generally believed existence at this time of
> desperate, reckless and lawless men in our midst,
> banded together for mutual support and living by
> felonious and predatory pursuits, regarding nei-
> ther life nor property in their career, and at the
> same time for men to parade the streets armed with
> repeating rifles and six-shooters and demand that
> the chief of police and his assistants should be
> disarmed is a proposition both monstrous and
> startling![17]

Spicer did not mince words. And, although Mayor Clum and
the Tombstone City Council had suspended Virgil as city marshal,
Virgil's actions on the day of the shootout received the highest
praise from his boss, U. S. Marshal of Arizona Territory Crawley
P. Dake. Marshal Dake wrote to the Acting Attorney General of the
United States, S. F. Phillips, on December 3, 1881, outlining the

history of the Cochise County problems and the recent shootout in the streets of Tombstone:

> Hereafter my deputies will not be interfered with in hunting down Stage Robbers, Mail Robbers, Train Robbers, Cattle thieves, and all that class of murdering *banditti* on the border. I am proud to report that I have some of the best and bravest men in my employ in this hazardous business—men who are trusty and tried, and who strike fear into the hearts of these outlaws.[18]

Some residents of Tombstone in 1881 were undoubtedly confused as to the real authority, the correct spokesman for law and order on the day of the shootout. Virgil Earp was the city chief of police of Tombstone, and Johnny Behan was the sheriff of Cochise County. Chief of Police Earp considered himself the supreme law dispenser in his city; furthermore, he despised the cowboy-loving ways of Sheriff Behan. However, Virgil Earp had more than the Tombstone chief of police position going for him. In his testimony before Justice Spicer, Virgil was asked what position he held on the day of the shooting:

> Chief of Police of Tombstone and Deputy United States Marshal, and was acting as such on those days.

Virgil was not known as a quick-tempered fellow, so the listing of his lawman credentials lent much credibility to his testimony.

As a result of the hearings, therefore, the Earps were cleared, the cowboys castigated, and Sheriff Behan and Ike Clanton were even further humiliated. But the days of the Earp domination were over. Virgil was out of a job, on suspension. Also, although Spicer had cleared them legally, there was evidence that the townspeople were becoming wary and weary of the tough stand the Earps took. Although the Clantons and McLaurys were cowboys, i.e., part of the rustling crowd, there is no evidence that Tom and Frank and Billy Clanton had any evil intent on the day of the shootout. In a way, they were the victims of Earp wrath, brought on by the drunken blustering of Ike Clanton.

Lest some of what appears in this chapter seems overly kind to the Earps, consider what other more objective, or more bitter, reporters have to say. Clara Brown, Tombstone correspondent for the *San Diego Union* provided almost weekly accounts of the mining city, describing new buildings, social and cultural affairs, mining progress, and political feuds to her San Diego readers. She viewed the funeral and wrote of the brass band and its long line of carriages, footmen, and horsemen:

> A stranger viewing the funeral cortege, which was the largest ever seen in Tombstone, would have thought that some person esteemed by the entire camp was being conveyed to his final resting place. . . .but such a public manifestation of sympathy from so large a portion of the residents of the camp seemed reprehensible when it is remembered that the deceased were nothing more or less than thieves. It is but a few weeks since all three were found to be implicated in the stealing of cattle and horses.[19]

William R. Breakenridge, deputy sheriff of Cochise County, and appointee of Sheriff Behan, had some of the sheriff's timidity and overall caution. Breakenridge disliked the Earps and was a close associate of the cowboy faction; in particular, he admired Johnny Ringo and Curly Bill. Breakenridge's account, *Helldorado*, although intended to disparage the Earps, actually agreed with Clara Brown's assessment of the Clantons and the McLaurys.

Breakenridge explained the rustling of Mexican cattle, the carousing in and around Galeyville and Charleston, and the large number of Texas cowhands who gravitated towards this outlaw life:

> Their leaders were John Ringo and William Brocius, better known as Curly Bill. . . .The Clantons looked after the rustlers' interests on the San Pedro, as a lot of stolen stock was brought from Mexico down the river, and there was no one watching the line for smugglers. The McLaurys looked after the stock brought up from Mexico through Agua Prieta, where Douglas now stands, into the Sulphur Spring Valley. . . .The stage robbers, hold-up men, and other outlaws that made these places a refuge, included Frank Stillwell, Pete Spencer, Zwing Hunt, Billy Grounds, Jim Crane, Harry Head, Billy Leonard, and their followers whose names I have forgotten. At this time the outlaws, rustlers, stage robbers, and certain of the gamblers were good friends.[20]

Deputy Sheriff Breakenridge helped explain why the Earps, Mayor Clum, and Justice Spicer may all have been prejudiced, predetermined to think the worst of the Clantons and the McLaurys. They were crooks. Subsequent events confirmed this.

FOOTNOTES

1. Turner, *O. K. Corral Inquest*, p. 32-33.
2. 'Ibid., p. 191.
3. Clum, *Arizona Historical Review*, 1929, p. 46.
4. Turner, *O. K. Corral Inquest*, p. 192.
5. Ibid., p. 162, Wyatt's testimony, in which he claims he shouted at Ike, "You damned dirty cow thief!"
6. Ibid.
7. Ibid., p. 54; testimony of Wm. Allen.
8. Turner, *O. K. Corral Inquest*, p. 163.
9. Ibid., pp. 192-93.
10. Ibid., p. 181-88; Sills testimony.
11. Ibid., p. 193; Virgil's testimony.
12. Ibid., pp. 136-54; Behan testimony.
13. Testimony of Fuller, Claiborne, and Allen is included in the *Inquest*.
14. Ibid., p. 193; Virgil's testimony.
15. Ibid., p. 164; Wyatt's testimony.
16. Ibid., p. 192; Virgil's testimony.
17. Ibid., pp. 217-26; Spicer summation.
18. The letter is in the Earp Papers, Special Collections, University of Arizona, Tucson.
19. San Diego *Union*, November 3, 1881.
20. Breakenridge, *Helldorado*, pp. 105, 135-37.

VI: VENGEANCE AND VENDETTA

The shootout, as well as the subsequent hearings that cleared the Earp faction of any wrongdoing, did nothing to end the smoldering feud between the Earps and the cowboys. More blood was to flow than had during the shootout. Who was responsible for the bloodletting has never been established, but logic and circumstantial evidence force the reader to conclude that Ike Clanton, and perhaps Sheriff Johnny Behan, either knew about the affair, or had a hand in planning it.

Within days of the shootout rumors hit Tombstone that if the Earps were freed, the cowboys would take revenge, going so far as to establish a hit list. Therefore, as soon as Justice Spicer's decision was known, the conspirators got to work. The Earps, Justice Spicer, Mayor Clum, and Attorney Tom Fitch and perhaps some others received death notes in the mail.[1]

The first recipient of the cowboy wrath was Mayor Clum. On the evening of December 14, Clum took the eight o'clock stage for Benson with five other passengers. Four miles out of Tombstone,

147

a band of armed men attacked and fired on the stage as it was going down a slight grade. About twenty shots were fired. One of the horses was felled, and the driver put the whip to the remainder of the team, even though he, too, was hit in the leg. The bandits—or assassins—did not pursue the stage.

The stage stopped, and Clum got out. He later wrote:

> As I looked at the coach with its sidelights, I realized that my presence in the coach only jeopardized the other passengers. I was much better off with my feet on the ground. . .and no sidelights. I struck off through the mesquite and cactus. . .on foot. After a precarious trek. . .in and out of ravines. . .I arrived at the Grand Central quartz mill about 1 o'clock a.m. The mill superintendent was a friend, and I told him my story. He telephoned to Tombstone that I was safe.[2]

The boldness of the attack—on the Mayor of Tombstone—meant that the death threats must be taken seriously. The news of the attempt on Clum's life made page one in the San Diego *Union* and the Los Angeles *Herald* of December 16, an indication of the widespread interest in the Earp-cowboy feud.

Justice Spicer revealed that he had received a death threat in the mail, but he decided to confront the issue. He had the letter published in the *Epitaph*, along with a stinging challenge to the "rabble" and "cowards" who hid from direct challenge.[3]

Virgil Earp, ex-marshal of Tombstone, was the next to encounter the cowboy revenge. The account of the attack as published in the Los Angeles *Herald* of December 30 agrees with all other reports:

Last night [December 28] about half-past 11 o'clock, as the United States Deputy Marshal was crossing Fifth street, between the Oriental saloon and Eagle brewery, and when in the middle of the street, he was fired upon with double-barreled shotguns, loaded with buckshot, by three men concealed in an unfinished building diagonally across on Allen street. Five shots were fired in rapid succession. Marshal Earp was wounded in the left arm just above the elbow, producing a longitudinal fracture of the bone. One shot struck him above the groin, coming out near the spine. The wounds are very dangerous, possibly mortal. The men ran through the rear building and escaped in the darkness, back of the Vizina hoisting works.

A near-witness to the event was mining engineer George Parsons. He was temporarily living with Dr. George Goodfellow, above the Golden Eagle Brewery, while recovering from injuries received during the city fire. Dr. Goodfellow had just left the room, when a "terrible noise" erupted from the gunfire. Parsons at first thought Goodfellow had been hit, but he had crossed the street moments before Virgil. Parsons reported that Virgil did not fall after being hit and that he recrossed the street to the Oriental. From there Virgil was taken to the Cosmopolitan Hotel. Parsons heard cries of "There they go," and "Head them off," but without City Marshal Virgil Earp in charge, Parsons had little hope for effective police action.

Parsons ran to the hospital to get Dr. Goodfellow, and they went to the now heavily guarded Cosmopolitan where they had trouble getting by the guards to enter Virgil's room. Parsons' diary entries:

149

He was easy. Told him I was sorry for him.
"It's Hell, isn't it!" said he. His wife was troubled.
"Never mind, I've got one arm left to hug you
with," he said.[4]

The next day, Virgil's arm was worked over, and the elbow
joint had to be removed.

Parsons' theory as to the responsible parties would have
surprised nobody in Tombstone:

It is surmised that Ike Clanton, "Curly Bill"
and [W. R.] McLaury did the shooting. Bad state of
affairs here. Something will have to be done.

Ike Clanton's hat was found near the scene of the shooting,
and other suspects included Johnny Ringo, Pete Spence, Frank
Stillwell, and Johnny Barnes. In fact, anyone with cowboy
associations could be placed in the "probably suspect" category.

An indication of the chaos then prevailing in Tombstone was
that nobody in the city had reason to believe that the police or
Sheriff Behan would or could track down the ambushers. Wyatt
Earp certainly had no faith in these lawmen. On the day following
the shooting of Virgil, Wyatt telegraphed U. S. Marshal Crawley
P. Dake in Prescott:

Virgil Earp was shot by a concealed assassin
last night. The wound is considered fatal. Telegraph me appointment with power to appoint
deputies. Local authorities have done nothing. The
lives of other citizens have been threatened.[5]

Marshal Dake immediately telegraphed the commission making Wyatt Earp a deputy U. S. marshal; the oath was administered by Deputy U. S. Marshal Virgil Earp, lying in what many felt was his death bed.[6]

Virgil was weak from the wounds and subsequent operation on his arm, and for several weeks he was in serious to critical condition. His left arm was permanently crippled by this midnight attack.

Virgil Earp had little to do with subsequent events in Tombstone. He recovered slowly from his wounds, and was gradually able to walk around the house and in the street. Morgan, too, was still recovering from shootout wounds, and he and Virgil spent quite a bit of time together during January and February.

Deputy U. S. Marshal Wyatt Earp was busy, not only with posses trying to track down the cowboy assassins, but he was also involved in legal hassles with Sheriff Behan and Ike Clanton. Forced by Wyatt to seek refuge in the county jail, Clanton once again pressed murder charges against the Earp faction. Judge Henry Lucas released Wyatt, Doc, and Morgan on a writ of habeas corpus. Virgil had not been taken into custody because of his wounds. This further decision to free the Earps meant additional bitterness from the cowboys, and new rumors of death lists were heard in Tombstone.

In spite of these rumors, on March 18 Morgan Earp insisted on attending a theatrical performance of "Stolen Kisses." Later that evening Wyatt reluctantly accompanied Morgan to Hatch's billiard parlor to watch as Morgan and Bob Hatch played a game.

Towards eleven o'clock, two shots were fired through the window of a rear door. The first shot slammed Morgan in the right side, penetrating his spinal column, left his body, then wounded bystander George A. B. Berry in the leg. The second shot blasted the wall inches above Wyatt's head. Wyatt, totally involved with attending his younger brother Morgan, did not bother seeking the midnight ambushers. Morgan, surrounded now by a crowd, died an hour later.[7] The San Diego *Union* of March 31 reported on the sad final minutes:

> The man was surrounded by his brothers and their wives, whose grief was intense. He whispered some words to Wyatt, which have not been given to the public, but spoke aloud only once, when his companions endeavored to raise him to his feet: "Don't, boys, don't," he said, "I can't stand it; I have played my last game of pool."

The West became a different place when Morgan Earp died. The famous shootout itself had gotten Tombstone—and the Earps—national notoriety. Now Wyatt would move to a larger stage. Brother Virgil was crippled for life, and brother Morgan was dead. Deputy U. S. Marshal Wyatt Earp made a vow to set things right for the Earp family by slaying the men responsible. No longer waiting for Sheriff Johnny Behan or any other agent of the law, Wyatt set out on a personal vendetta without parallel in the American West.

To pinpoint the exact cowboys responsible is almost impossible, unless new evidence surfaces. However, in recent decades a series of letters has become available which implies strongly that Will McLaury, the attorney and brother of the dead McLaury boys, bankrolled the assassins. It will be remembered that Will was admitted by Justice Spicer to participate in the hearings as "friendly counsel" during the hearings about the shootout. The hearings did not bring the result Will McLaury wanted, and it appears that his anger and bitterness led him to pay off certain cowboys to shoot at Mayor Clum, Marshal Earp, and Morgan Earp.

The four letters written by Will McLaury are in the New-York

Historical Society, and although they contain fascinating insights into the Tombstone scene, they fit more with the development of the Wyatt Earp legend. One paragraph, though, from his letter of April 13, 1884, to his father, gives the flavor and motivation behind Will McLaury's actions:

> My experience out there [Tombstone] has been very unfortunate as to my health and badly injured me as to money matters. And none of the results have been satisfactory. The only result is the death of Morgan and crippling of Virgil Earp.[8]

Through a bit of luck, Marshal Wyatt Earp soon had all the information he needed to act. Pete Spence [or, Spencer] had, for various reasons, beaten his wife, Marietta. Supposedly they had quarreled when she found out he had been a participant in Morgan's assassination. Marietta Spence told all to a coroner's jury, naming the assassins as Pete Spence, Frank Stilwell, Florentine Cruz [Indian Charlie?], a German named Freis, and another Indian, "Name Unknown"; the latter was most likely Hank Swilling.

The first thing for the Earps to do, though, was to get their dependents out of town, back to the Nicholas Earp home in Colton, California. After vigorous talks, the family decided that Virgil and Allie, James and his wife Bessie, Morgan's wife Lou, and Wyatt's wife Mattie would leave on the train from Tucson. Morgan's coffin would be part of the entourage. Some of the party boarded the train at Contention, others at Tucson. A few accounts stated that Wyatt had arranged as escorts to Tucson fellow gunslingers Doc Holliday, Warren Earp, Sherman McMasters, Texas Jack Vermillion, and Turkey Creek Jack Johnson.[9]

The first Earp revenge was at hand. While in the train station in Tucson on the evening of March 20, 1882, Virgil and Wyatt saw

Frank Stilwell and another man, apparently Ike Clanton. Stilwell may have been there to meet a man who was to be a witness at Stilwell's upcoming trial, or he may have been there to cause further trouble for the Earps.

What happened next is not known precisely, as Wyatt gave several varying accounts over the years. For Frank Stilwell, the details did not matter. His body was found near the railroad tracks the next morning, about 100 yards north of Porter's Hotel. This had been no duel, no man-to-man showdown in the streets of Tucson. The coroner's report specified a wound under the armpit, a rifle ball in the upper left arm, buckshot in the stomach, a rifle ball in the right leg, and buckshot in the left leg. Stilwell could have died of lead poisoning.

Wyatt gladly took credit for the carnage, but he had most likely been helped by Doc Holliday and Warren Earp. Also, some accounts hint that the other party with Stilwell could have been Hank Swilling, rather than Ike Clanton. In a newspaper interview years later, Sheriff Bob Paul stated that while the train was standing in Tucson, "Stilwell was seen standing on a gravel car peeking in the window of the car that Virgil Earp was in. Wyatt Earp and the balance of the escort started after him, overtook him and killed him."[10]

So, while Virgil Earp headed the family party to California, Deputy U. S. Marshal Wyatt Earp led his gang of deputies—McMasters, Doc Holliday, Warren Earp, Texas Jack Vermillion, and Turkey Creek Jack Johnson back towards Tombstone. Frank Stilwell was dead, but there were others who would pay for the killing of Morgan Earp.

A difficulty with this plan was that U. S. Deputy Marshal Wyatt Earp was now wanted by the law. He took pride in killing Stilwell. But the authorities in Tucson did not share his feelings. The coroner's jury there found that Stilwell had been killed by Wyatt

154

Frank Stilwell. Arizona Historical Society

Earp and his party, and the sheriff of Pima County was given an arrest warrant for Wyatt Earp. This was Sheriff Bob Paul, a long-time friend of Wyatt, but a tough law-and-order man who resented Wyatt's invasion of his county and to carry out the revenge killing.

But all of that is part of the Wyatt Earp story, and our interests here are with the career of Virgil Earp. With useless arm in a sling by his side, Virgil could gaze out of the train window at passing Arizona landscapes he might never see again, as the Earp funeral convoy sped towards Morgan Earp's final resting place in California.

Motivation and guilt will be forever argued in the case of the Earps and the cowboys. Wyatt's vendetta would cloud the Earp reputation for a time, but Virgil's reputation never suffered from his service in Tombstone. The cowardly shootings of Virgil and Morgan were done by, or at least encouraged by, the cowboy faction. This was not secret. However, such knowledge did not change many minds in Cochise County about the relative merits of either party.

Again, Clara Brown of the San Diego *Union*, as perceptive as any correspondent who wrote about Tombstone, could not penetrate the layers of thoughts and deeds that helped define these differences. Her comments in the issue of February 4, 1882:

> One would suppose that all peaceable, honest men would denounce and oppose the outlaws, for they are virtually such, but a large proportion of otherwise good citizens waste a surprising amount of sympathy on them, in the face of evidence against them which ought to be thoroughly convincing. The maudlin sympathy and offers of pecuniary assistance offered the assassin Guiteau

156

[President Garfield's assassin] by certain individu-
als is the only parallel case which I can recall. ·

FOOTNOTES

1. Those threatened by anonymous letters included the Earps, Doc Holliday, Justice Spicer, and perhaps Attorney Tom Fitch; *Weekly Arizona Miner*, December 30, 1881.
2. Clum's account is in *Arizona Historical Review*, 1929, pp. 57-58.
3. *Epitaph*, December 13, 1881.
4. Chafin (ed.), *Parsons*, entry of December 28, 1881, p. 163.
5. *Weekly Arizona Miner*, December 30, 1881.
6. Mentioned in *Phoenix Herald*, December 30, 1881.
7. The San Diego *Union* of March 22, 23, and 24 carried articles on Morgan's death; one was entitled, "A Bloody Sequel." For details of Morgan's death, see Douglas D. Martin, *Tombstone's Epitaph* (Albuquerque, 1951), pp. 217-18, and Chafin (ed.), *Parsons*, 1882, pp. 24-25.
8. The originals of the four Will McLaury letters are in the New-York Historical Society; copies are in the Arizona Historical Society, Tucson.
9. See Turner, *Earps Talk*, p. 220, and Martin, *Tombstone's Epitaph*, p. 219 for the trip from Tombstone to Colton.
10. Paul interview in *Tombstone Prospector*, March 3, 1898. Details of Stilwell's life, and his bloody death, are in the San Diego *Union* of March 25, 1882, and *Arizona Weekly Citizen*, April 2, 1882.

VII: CITY MARSHAL, COLTON, CALIFORNIA

The first order of business once the traveling party had reached California was to bury Morgan. According to Allie:

> We got to Nicholas Porter and Grandma Earp's
> place in Colton all right and buried Morg near a hill
> there. It was sad for all of us. I watched the coffin
> bein' lowered and Virge tryin to stand up during
> the last prayer. . . .But when I looked at Lou whose
> husband was being buried, at Mattie whose hus-
> band [Wyatt] had left her for that strumpet, and
> thought of Kate whose husband [Doc Holliday]
> had never treated her as his wife neither, I quit
> feelin' sorry for myself. I was the luckiest of all the
> Earp women. I still had Virge.[1]

Allie may have had Virge, but it was a Virge in pain and with parts missing. Before they really settled down in Colton, Virgil made some contacts through Wells, Fargo in San Francisco, and in late May he and Allie went there for medical treatment. He had further surgery on the arm, which left him permanently crippled, and with the arm a bit shorter than it had been. The Los Angeles *Times* of May 28 mentioned the loss of about six inches of bone in the arm. "In conversation Earp admitted that his party killed Stilwell." Neither then, nor later, did Virgil or Wyatt deny, or show any regret for having killed Stillwell, the ambusher of their brother Morgan.

On May 28, the San Diego *Union* provided a few additional details of Earp family doings, stating that Virgil had heard from Wyatt and Warren, who were heavily involved in posses and in pursuit of the cowboys and their friends. The *Union* quoted the local Colton newspaper as saying that Nicholas Earp and sons James and Virgil were residents, and "a quieter, more law-abiding family we do not often meet, and from them we learn all that they ask for themselves and brothers is simple justice."

In a few months Virgil went to San Francisco for a further inspection of his arm. Perhaps Virgil felt that San Francisco might appeal to him for a variety of reasons. The Phoenix *Arizona Gazette* of July 27, 1882, reported that he was "in business in San Francisco." However, the *Gazette* of August 10 clarified the business, and no doubt is the reason why that city quickly lost its charm for the Earps:

> Virgil Earp, of Tombstone notoriety, was arrested last Tuesday in San Francisco, on a charge of dealing faro. Over $1,000 and a "lay out" was captured with him.

Virgil's timing was bad. The Los Angeles *Times* of August 4 and

Nick Earp was active in Colton, California, where in addition to running a saloon he also served as justice of the peace. Colton Semti-Tropic, November 27, 1880

5 announced two big raids on faro rooms, and apparently Los Angeles as well as San Francisco had decided to crack down on gambling.

Virgil and Allie decided to return to the quiet of Colton, and settled on the outskirts of town. Allie described their place as not much, "just a stretch of cactus with some trees along the creek." They had little need of acreage or numerous outbuildings. Virgil was in bad condition, having been near death from the wounds of the shootout, which was followed by the blasting of his arm and

161

leg during the ambush. It would take Allie several years to nurse Virgil back to a reasonable health.

In addition to James and Bessie and Virgil and Allie, Nick and Virginia had other relatives living nearby. Daughter Adelia, who had married Bill Edwards, lived in Colton for a time, then moved to nearby Mt. Vernon. For some years, then, this group formed the basis of the Earp clan in San Bernardino County, with Warren being a frequent visitor and resident, and Wyatt stopping by occasionally.[2]

During this period Colton was one of the busiest little towns in the West, on the brink of greatness—or so many residents believed. Nick Earp had moved his family there from Temescal, near Riverside, in 1880, because he believed in the future of the community. He had judged correctly. Nick opened a business, the Gem Saloon, which featured the "best Tom and Jerry in town." He quickly became a local "character," a fixture, in Colton and in San Bernardino County.[3]

The settlement of Colton was sixty miles from Los Angeles, with a population of about 2,000 at this time. The town had a few newspapers, telegraph, telephone, and Wells, Fargo offices, three hotels, two banks, churches, and schools, cemeteries, and merchant houses. It also had the Southern Pacific Railroad. And in 1883, the year after Virgil had come to town, the California Southern Railroad, a branch of the Atlantic and Pacific, crossed the Southern Pacific tracks in Colton. The significance of this is baldly stated in *Place's Southern California Guide Book* for 1886:

> Colton is destined to be a railroad center, for here the trans-continental railways cross each other—something that does not occur at any other place in the United States.

162

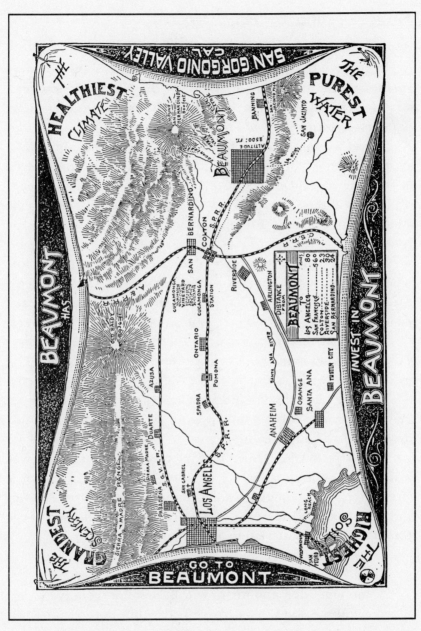

Justice Nick Earp and Chief of Police Virgil Earp were kept busy in Colton, crossroads of two major railroad lines. Natural History Museum, Los Angeles

In other words, with the east-west traffic of the Southern Pacific and the north-south pattern of the California Southern, almost every rail traveler in the Southwest passed through Colton; not even Los Angeles could boast such attention.[4]

Therefore, important railroad offices were located in Colton, as well as those of Wells, Fargo. In a few years, the federal government would decide to place the Mission Indian Agency office in Colton, thus making Colton the supply, legal, and administrative center for all the Southern California Indian reserves.[5]

For a few years, it was rumored, even encouraged, that Colton would replace San Bernardino as the county seat. Colton was the coming place, due to this rail focus. The Los Angeles *Times* of January 22, 1886, referred to the interest in Colton, "The fever is spreading." At that time, each day there were twelve passenger and eight freight trains going through and stopping at Colton. Few places in the world had such traffic. Colton was also in the center of a thriving fruit growing and packing region, and on nearby Mt. Slover, cement quarries would provide work for the community for more than half a century.

The Earps joined in the life of the active community, as well as in county affairs. While Nick ran the Gem Saloon, James was in business also, operating a boarding house. In August of 1884, Nick and Virgil decided to test the political waters. The San Diego *Union* carried this news item on August 21:

> N. P. Earp, of Colton, is the Democratic nominee for Auditor of San Bernardino county, while his son Virgil Earp, of Tombstone notoriety, is an aspirant for office in that county, on the Republican side.

164

It was obvious by now that Virgil would not only recover, but that he apparently would also be able to live an active life. Nick was a true-blue Democrat, even though his sons Virgil and Wyatt were lifelong Republicans. Although Nick had first come to San Bernardino in 1864, he had spent only a few years there before returning to the Midwest. He returned in 1880 to San Bernardino but by 1884 he still had not captured enough local enthusiasm to get elected. Virgil, who had also been in California in 1866-67, was not well known locally, although his name and reputation were bandied about.

The 1884 announcement made in the San Diego *Union* was not quite accurate. Virgil may have thought of testing the waters and running for sheriff of San Bernardino County, but he did not do so. He did, however, get active in local Republican politics. In mid-August, he was elected a precinct delegate to attend the Republican Party County Convention, which was held in San Bernardino on August 20. At the convention, the rumors of Virgil's candidacy for sheriff died quickly. Three men were considered for the post, but Virgil's name never surfaced. However, Virgil did at least establish his credentials as a resident interested in local politics, something in the Earp blood. By November, Nick seemed to have gotten a better local base; he ran for justice of the peace in Colton Township and was easily elected.[6]

There was no doubt now that Virgil was seeking the active life. An entry in the San Diego *Union* of September 6, 1885, stated that "Virgil Earp, one of the famous Earps of Arizona, is in town." This meant cards, both faro and poker. From this point on, Wyatt, too, became a frequent visitor to San Diego, living there for a few years in the late 1880s. Virgil may have been able to use only one hand, but he remained dedicated to the green cloth.

Virgil Earp was no free-loader, and having recovered somewhat from the disastrous shootings in Tombstone, decided it was

165

time to bring in a steady income in Colton. In early summer of 1886, he opened a detective agency there, hoping that his reputation would lead to a few assignments. A newspaper notice gave as reference "any prominent citizen of Kansas, New Mexico, Arizona or California."[7] The *Weekly Journal-Miner* in Prescott continued to chronicle Virgil's doings, and reported in its issue of June 23 that Virgil was "running a detective bureau in Colton, California."

Allie remembered a few jobs, one in particular related to Virgil's role in finding a stage robber and placing him in the county jail.[8]

Politics interfered with Virgil's budding detective agency. On July 2, 1886, Virgil Earp was elected constable of the village of Colton.[9] Nick ran again for justice of the peace and won. There were many hot issues in Colton at that time, including a vote for incorporation that failed. One of the most amazing aspects of the victories of Nick and Virgil Earp is that Colton was not a wide-open town. Bordellos were non-existent, and liquor was discouraged, with very few licensed places. Among those elected to office were Nick Earp, owner of the Gem Saloon, and Virgil Earp, gambler *par-excellence*.

In the good old days in Lamar, Barton County, Missouri, Nick Earp had been justice of the peace, and son Wyatt Earp had been constable. They were law and order there, and the old one-two kept both of them in good financial condition. Wyatt would arrest someone, Nick would fine someone, and both would share in the fee distribution. Colton was to become the good old days all over again, this time with Virgil doing the arresting, Nick doing the fining, and the new father and son team sharing in the fines.

The Earp boys spent thousands of hours in saloons, yet there was never any indication that Virgil or Wyatt loved the bottle. They thrived on the atmosphere, enjoyed the talk, and were both inveterate gamblers. Nick Earp, saloon owner, never appreciated vomit on the floor, or having a drunk disturb the community. Constable Virgil Earp and Justice of the Peace Nicholas Earp never violated the trust of the Colton citizens who frowned on alcohol. The following entry from the San Bernardino *Weekly Times* of October 16, 1886, is typical of the Earp approach in Colton:

> Judge Earp, of Colton, is doing good work in the temperance cause by imposing heavy and frequent fines on drunks in that city.

Although Colton was a small community, its location at such a major rail junction led to some criminal activities, and the presence of a few criminal types, which were not usually found in towns of 2,000. Drunks were a problem, as well as the occasional opium user, child molester, petty thief, or merchant selling booze to the Indians. Justice Nicholas Earp, in May of 1887, fined one fellow $20 and slapped him in the county jail for twenty days for indecently exposing himself to a young girl.[10]

A severe problem for Colton, one that lasted for decades, was that of the tramps. The type and degree of problem was pointed out by the San Bernardino *Weekly Times* of February 12, 1887:

> Constable Earp brought up from Colton this morning eight tramps who had been sentenced to ten days each by Justice Earp of Colton. They were captured asleep in a box car and the tax payers have got to put up some ten to fifteen dollars each for them in Justice fees, constable fees, board and attention.

The Constable Earp, who was grappling with doors of boxcars

and eight to ten vagrants, was one-armed Virgil. His useless left arm did not seem to lessen his efficiency or ability as a peace officer. His sister Adelia recalled an incident in Colton in 1887 when a few swaggering young drunks made a remark about Virgil's crippled arm:

> In about a tick of the clock, he [the drunk] was off his feet, right up off the street and onto the sidewalk, and pretty hard up against the wall, spread-eagled. Virgil did all this in one move, with one arm. He sure was a strong feller! He just frisked this young drunk a bit rough and pushed him away, and said "Now you just run along home, boy."[11]

Virgil had killed a few men in his duties as a peace officer, in Prescott and in Tombstone, but he solved most disputes with a kind, firm word, or a stern warning. If these methods did not produce the desired action, Virgil and Wyatt Earp performed their most efficient law-and-order technique, that of buffaloing, or slamming the barrel of a pistol across the opponent's forehead. Even one-handed Virgil could still perform that operation with ease.

The citizens of Colton felt comfortable with Virgil as constable. On July 11, 1887, Colton had its most important election to date. In a push for status, and in an effort to outshine the City of San Bernardino, the citizens of Colton voted to incorporate as a city; the vote was 116 to 57 in favor. Among the officers voted in that day for the new city was "V. W. Earp, Marshal." Virgil received 109 votes to 61 for Wm. Brown and 1 for L. S. Abel. According to the Los Angeles *Evening Express* of July 12, "There is great rejoicing over the result." Supposedly, the big issue in this

168

mostly dry town was temperance. It seems that the Earps, as non-temperance as could be, had no difficulty working in an environment of the temperance crowd.

The people of Colton had been permitted by state law to vote for incorporation as a city of the sixth class, meaning an unincorporated area with less than 3,000 inhabitants.

A few days after the election, the San Bernardino *Daily Times* printed this notice:

> V. W. Earp, the newly elected City Marshal, sports a gold badge that was presented to him by the Wells, Fargo express company for services done at Tombstone, A.T., years ago, when he was Marshal of that city. It is a beauty and cost in the neighborhood of eighty dollars.[12]

This was not only a fine tribute, but put to rest the absurd rumors of the Earps' being involved in stage robberies and theft of Wells, Fargo treasure boxes in Arizona. The presentation of the gold badge was made by John Valentine, vice-president of Wells, Fargo, on the recommendation of Fred Dodge, an intimate of the Earp brothers and the Wells, Fargo undercover man in Tombstone.

One incident, shortly after Virgil became city marshal, proved embarrassing, but at least it establishes that Colton had a jail. The "arch-fiend" Tom Gormley was wanted in Los Angeles on a rape charge. Marshal Earp telegrammed the Los Angeles chief of police, stating that he had reason to believe "Ravisher" Gormley was in his jail. Detective Bosqui was sent out on the midnight train to escort Gormley back to Los Angeles. "He at once found Detective Earp, and together they repaired to the cell where the alleged Gormley lay a prisoner." It appears that Virgil Earp, "Colton's

169

> Marshal Virgil Earp arrested the arch-
> fiend, Tom Gormlee, at Colton last
> night, and he was sent to Los Angeles
> this morning. Officer Bosqui, of he lat-
> ter place, identified the low-lived rapist.

Enforcing the law means dealing with all sorts of crimes, all sorts of folks. San Bernardino Daily Times, July 20, 1887

famous detective," had misidentified the man, so Bosqui returned to Los Angeles empty handed.[13]

The Earp family fortunes had improved even more before the end of July. The new city board of trustees, at its first meeting on July 25, appointed Nicholas Earp as city recorder. So Nick, still a justice of the peace, had an additional income, and at the same time a new acknowledgement that he was a man to be reckoned with, somewhat, in the new city.

The San Bernardino *Daily Times* of July 30, 1887, had two interesting comments about Colton. Marshal Earp had visited the city that morning, and "his little salary is still going right on." The other brief note at least established what salary Virgil was getting:

> A few old fogies at Colton are kicking up a terrible muss over the salaries that have been established for the City Clerk and City Marshal of that burg. One gets fifty and the other seventy-five dollars. This is the result of trying to be a city when there is not enough people represented to defray the expenses.

But there was other publicity to counter the complaints about

170

their pay. Marshal Earp, and the City of Colton, were continually plagued with the tramp situation. This is the price the city paid for being a railroad center. Even in that era, tramps were aware of things like climate, often arriving in Southern California in time to winter. The Riverside *Morning Enterprise* a few years later outlined the habits of the tramps, who often traveled in groups "towards this inviting climate." There were tussles with trainmen, with local constables and sheriffs, and with railway detectives. None of the harassing slowed the tramp traffic. A winter in Colton was preferable, even then, to one in Chicago. The San Bernardino *Daily Times* of August 10, 1887, was overly optimistic on Marshal Earp's ability to solve the tramp question:

> Marshal Earp of Colton is making it very warm
> for the tramps and thieves that infest that place.
> Now let our people help the police, and run the
> gang out of this city.

The difficulty in dealing with the tramp problem was the danger of doing so evenhandedly. For example, the Los Angeles *Times* of October 19, 1888, titled an article, "Constables' Racket." It seems the Los Angeles constables and their deputies would go out of their way to seek and arrest tramps, just to collect the processing fees. It may have been that Virgil's enthusiasm in Colton for arresting tramps was related to the fees he and Justice of the Peace Nick Earp would share.

The Mission Consolidated Agency, the unit dealing with the Mission Indians of California, although headquartered at Colton, did not provide much work for Marshal Earp. The agent and a few clerks were stationed in Colton, only because of its rail connections, and not because of a large local Indian population. At Colton, the Indian agent had neither courts nor police, and had to rely on local legal agencies frequently. However, there were county and other federal officials, such as the county sheriff, and various deputy U. S. marshals. Most problems involved the liquor traffic, and there were dozens of arrests of merchants peddling alcohol, who spent a few days in jail in San Bernardino or Los Angeles. Marshal Earp's name does not appear in these records, although his Colton jail most likely housed some of the Indians and liquor merchants who were enroute to jail elsewhere.

In late August of 1887 an Indian was charged with rape near the town of Banning, which was east of Colton some twenty miles. The Indian claimed that he was innocent, and that he knew who the guilty party was. In any case, the Indian "was brought to the city [San Bernardino] last night by Marshal Earp of Colton, and placed in the County jail." Virgil, as City Marshal, had no jurisdiction near Banning, or anywhere outside of Colton; he most likely arrested the Indian in Colton, based on information received from elsewhere.[14] However, there have been hints, unsubstantiated, that Virgil Earp, city marshal of Colton, was also a deputy sheriff of San Bernardino County. Such a situation was not at all unusual, and could explain Virgil's presence in a legal capacity outside the city limits. In Tombstone, for example, while he was city marshal he was also a deputy U. S. marshal, giving him all sorts of territory to move in legally.

The duties of a law enforcement officer in Colton were much like those of law enforcement officers in San Francisco, St. Louis, or Newark. Crimes had much in common in different parts of the country. The difference in Colton was that Virgil handled everything himself, with no crew of deputies to send after tramps, fleeing rapists, petty thieves, slobbering drunks, wife beaters, check forgers, opium smokers, illegal booze peddlers, child molesters, or stage robbers.

The Bible for law enforcement officers at this time was W. S.

172

Harlow's *Duties of Sheriffs and Constables*, a San Francisco publication that had examples of all duties, printed forms, and even a schedule of fees. Some topics covered were militia exemptions from arrest, rescuing prisoners, service as auctioneer, suppression of riots, the fee book, inhumanity to prisoners, food and lodging for juries, arrests for fraud, service of bench warrants, and when arrests may be made at night.

The first business ordinance of the new City of Colton, which was passed on August 11, 1887, regulated licenses for peddlers, saloons, Chinese laundries, circuses, and so forth. The second ordinance, passed on September 2nd, concerned the licensing of wholesale and retail businesses. In April of 1888, a property tax law was passed. The issuing of all of these licenses and gathering in of tax receipts were jobs assigned to the city marshal; in addition, until early 1889, City Marshal Earp was also the city health officer.[15]

It is obvious by now that City Marshal Virgil Earp spent little of his time in the saddle pursuing villains or arresting wild-shooting cowboys. Colton was not a problem town, perhaps in part because of the presence of Virgil Earp. The Colton Board of Trustees Minutes for this period indicate that the routine, the boring, was much a part of Marshal Earp's tenure. A few of the bills he submitted were: 75 cents for lock and key for the jail; $4.25 for nails and meals for prisoners; $20.00 for sewer work. Another task:

> The Marshal was instructed to keep watch of
> the electric lights and note their burning. He was
> also instructed to procure a ballot box to be used
> at the next election.[16]

One of the more puzzling of law enforcement incidents

173

regarding City Marshal Virgil Earp occurred in August of 1887. Fred Dodge, the Wells, Fargo undercover specialist in Tombstone, was having troubles, especially with a recent train robbery at Pantano, just east of Tucson. Dodge had learned that two suspects, without horses, were headed towards Mountain Springs. Dodge needed help, rode into Benson and sent a telegram to Tombstone:

> About the first one that I heard from was Virgil Earp, who was in Tombstone—Charley Smith and I both wanted to see the Old Boy badly. He come down on the Stage and we met him at Benson. Virgil Earp had been in California Ever since they tried to assassinate him when he was City Marshal in Tombstone.

Dodge, always an Earp partisan, had been a room-mate in Tombstone with the deceased Morgan.

The chase after the robbers was not successful, but Dodge provided some interesting details of the chase. Dodge's scout, a Yaqui Indian named Manuel, became fascinated with Virgil's arm: "My God, Boss, what is the matter with that man?" Dodge had to stop the posse, and everyone dismounted while Dodge and Virgil explained about the shootout, and Virgil's arm:

> He [Manuel] felt of the arm, lifted it up, and let it fall, and was much impressed—and he and Virg become great friends. He looked out for Virg on all occasions and took care of Virg's horse for him on the whole trip—Virg was much amused at Manuel.

After the posse returned to Benson, Virgil Earp returned to

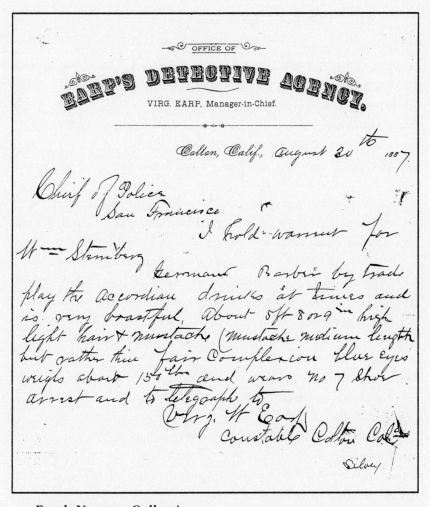

Frank Newton Collection

California, and Dodge reported that "it was some years later before I met Virg again."[17]

In the Wyatt Earp Papers there is a brief note that on October 25, 1887, in Colton, Phin Clanton was arrested and jailed by City Marshal Virgil Earp.[18] Although not so active as the other Clantons in the Tombstone cowboy circles, Phin was a younger brother of Ike Clanton, and also a brother of the deceased Billy Clanton,

175

riddled to death by Virgil and party at the famous shootout in Tombstone. However, this arrest of Phin in Colton seems impossible to have taken place. On October 7, 1887, Phin Clanton entered the gates of the Territorial Prison at Yuma, sentenced for his role in a robbery near Globe.

There was another election in Colton in April of 1888, and Virgil again entered his name for the position of marshal. He was easily reelected to a one-year term with the same rate of pay. The citizens of Colton saw no reason to change, and shortly after the election Nicholas Earp was reappointed city recorder.[19]

The peace officer situation in and around Colton was altered somewhat after Colton received city status in July of 1887. Now that the City of Colton had its own marshal, the remaining portion, the unincorporated areas of Colton Township, were served by two constables. Therefore, aside from various federal officials in the region, the peace officer authority was headed by the sheriff of San Bernardino County, then the marshals or police chiefs in the various cities, then the constables, a position usually reserved for unincorporated areas.

There was some indication that Virgil had his eye on another position. The Tucson *Arizona Daily Citizen* of July 21, 1888, reported that Virgil was trying to get the Republican nomination for sheriff of San Bernardino County. If so, his attempt was not successful. E. C. Seymour of San Bernardino received the nomination, and he was elected sheriff in the November election.

Virgil served out his second one-year term as city marshal, with apparently little excitement. No riots, series of bank robberies, outbreaks of violence, or other examples of lawlessness have come down to us from that part of Colton's history.

On March 9, 1889, the board of trustees received and accepted the resignation of Virgil W. Earp as city marshal. A month or so later, the city clerk checked the books and found that Virgil Earp

176

owed the city $12.27, on a tax collection he had not completed. The minutes of July 1, 1889, reflected that ex-Marshal Earp had taken care of the minor discrepancy. This was typical of Virgil's attention to detail; wherever he served, each penny, each slop bucket, each pair of handcuffs were carefully inventoried.

No ten-page letter exists which explains why Virgil Earp resigned as city marshal, but he was most likely bored. For example, the San Bernardino *Daily Courier* of May 9, 1889, during one of the periodic attempts to get the county seat shifted to Colton, reported:

> It will not do—Colton, we mean, will never do
> for a county seat. If San Bernardino is too rushing
> and bustling and noisy, Colton is too dull and
> dreary and monotonous.

That may have been exaggerated prose, but with some truth. If so, such a place was not for Virgil Earp. He needed excitement, wandering, the thrill of a crowded saloon, tables of green cloth, more open space. Virgil Earp, even while he was city marshal of Colton, had sought some of the more exciting life in the city of San Bernardino, just a few miles to the north.

The marshal's job had meant a decent income for Virgil, and while in that position he purchased a new home in town, at 528 West H Street. The county register of deeds book contains this entry for July 7, 1888:

> I, Virgil W. Earp, of the City of Colton, County
> of San Bernardino and State of California, for and
> in consideration of the love and affection which I
> bear towards my wife, and as an expression of my
> heartfelt gratitude to her for her constant, patient

and heroic attendance at my bedside while I lay
dangerously wounded at Tombstone, Arizona, do
grant unto my wife, Mrs. Alvira Earp, as her
separate estate, all that real property situated in the
City of Colton. . . .[Lots 5 and 6, Block 113]

Such testimonials are not part of many land entries, which
indicates the type of relationship that existed between Virgil and
Allie Earp.

The Earp family members are listed in the various city and
county directories during this era, and some of the entries are
puzzling, at least at first. Virgil was frequently listed as city marshal
and as a farmer. Even in Tombstone in the 1880 census he had been
listed as a farmer. Nick Earp was listed under a variety of
occupations, such as book agent, saloon keeper, but most often as
justice of the peace. Warren was listed in the 1889 county
directory as a "capitalist," living in the King House San Bernardino, and James in 1887-88 was shown as operator of the Club
Exchange, a saloon in San Bernardino.

Although Virgil resigned as city marshal in 1889, and shifted
his attention towards San Bernardino, he still kept an eye on
Colton affairs. He was a resident, and his father was still a
practicing justice there. In June of 1889, for example, Virgil served
on a coroner's jury, composed of "intelligent and enquiring men,"
in an abortion case.[20]

James, who had operated a boarding house in Colton for a
while, was in the saloon business in San Bernardino by 1887. A
Pacific Coast directory for 1886-87 lists Virgil "Erp" as proprietor
of the Bijou Theater at 78 Third Street in San Bernardino. The
Bijou opened in January of 1886, but Virgil's role in either its
founding or its operation, has not been determined. He may have
been a silent partner, as he was busy with law enforcement in

nearby Colton at that time, and the San Bernardino newspapers did not carry stories of Virgil as one of the Bijou personalities.

But Virgil and San Bernardino were well publicized in late December of 1889, as Joe Cotton and Jack Sullivan, boxers, went at it in San Bernardino's first professional fight. The *Daily Courier* ran several stories before and after the fight, which was held in the Opera House. There was "no vulgar blackguardism, no obscenity, no profanity, no brutality. . .for our part, we think that there is more demoralization in a bar-room row."

Virgil Earp was the manager of the affair, the referee, and may have been the inspiration behind the whole concept:

> The management of the affair, by Virgil Earp, was perfect. Absolute fair play was insisted upon. No outside interference was permitted. . . . Whether this is but the beginning of pugilistic sport in San Bernardino we do not know, but we know that if it is, and such affairs can be conducted as they were on Tuesday night, even the most rigid moralist can have little fault to find with them. Should there be any attempt made in the future to introduce degrading features into boxing-matches, it will not take San Bernardino long to suppress all such exhibitions, but that any such attempt will be made, while Virgil Earp is the manager of such affairs, is impossible. [21]

The match lasted 32 rounds, and Sullivan won in the crowd-pleasing event.

The days following were filled with boxing hype, as Cotton, the loser, wanted another bout. He blamed the loss on his seconds,

179

but felt that in another match he could win, "providing Mr. Virg. Earp will again act as referee."

The fight had received good publicity and had been well attended, so no one could give a reason why a second bout should not be held. It was so arranged, for January 18, again in the Opera House, and Virgil Earp would again officiate. Sullivan was quoted as saying that "it suits him exactly, as two of the Earp boys have refereed for him in two of his hardest fights." This would most likely refer to Wyatt, who had a long and controversial history as a boxing referee.

The first bout in San Bernardino should have been the last, because the rematch was a fraud. The fix was on, and it was obvious to the crowd, who booed throughout. Apparently the boxers had gotten together and agreed that Sullivan would fake, not fight. Supposedly, Cotton was to lose, but by fouling Sullivan:

> Mr. Earp, who saw how things were going, refused to be a party to such a foul fooling of the audience, and would not notice a foul, upon which Cotton threw off his gloves. No man in San Bernardino would pay five cents to see either Sullivan or Cotton, or both, fight again.[22]

San Bernardino may have said farewell to boxing, but Virgil did not. He remained interested in the sport and would arrange and referee matches elsewhere in the future.

Virgil's next business foray in San Bernardino was in 1890, when he opened a gambling hall on the second floor, above what later became the Isis Theater; this was on 3rd Street, between D and E Streets, in what was known as the Saterwhite Building.

Harry Allison, later County Clerk, recalled that as a youth he delivered telegrams to Virgil and other gamblers in the second story rooms. Allison remembered card tables, dice games, even a roulette wheel, but apparently Virgil did not have a bar at that time; a year or so later he did have liquor:

> Virgil was a gentleman. He had me take off my
> hat and hold up the message whenever I entered.
> . . .He always taught me to say, "Yes, sir," or "No,
> sir."

Allison was also subject to periodic preaching by Virgil, who would tell him, "Young man, you never win at gambling!" This was advice that Virgil obviously never followed; his death would come when he was in the employ of a gambling house.[23]

In 1890 Virgil had health problems, complaining of soreness in his wounded arm and back, and of "neuralgia of the stomach." He applied for a veteran's pension that year, based on his Civil War service, and on the fact that his disabilities were received in Arizona "in the discharge of my duties as U. S. Deputy Marshal and Chief of Police." The San Francisco office of the U. S. Pension Office approved the request, and Virgil received a 12/18ths disability, for which he received $12 a month for the rest of his life.[24]

For a month or two during this period Virgil got the moving feeling again, and set down at the Cosmopolitan Hotel in San Luis Obispo, California, an ocean town midway between Los Angeles and San Francisco. He officially changed his place of residence to San Luis Obispo in October, 1891.

No beach comber, he, although the *San Luis Opispo Tribune* of September 11 mentioned that Mr. and Mrs. Virgil Earp "will spend a month or two at the beach." Virgil was really following the county fair racing circuit. He had just gambled on the horses at Santa Maria, to the north, and the San Luis Obispo races were

181

to open in late September. This, not Pacific waves, was the kind of action Virgil craved. Within a few months Virgil and Allie were back in San Bernardino, but still restless.[25]

If Colton had become dull, San Bernardino, because of its size, did offer Virgil a few more amusements, such as gambling, saloon keeping, and arranging boxing matches. But San Bernardino was not a frontier community, which seemed to have some special appeal for Virgil. In the 1893 county directory, Virgil was listed as a saloonkeeper, but the name of the saloon was not listed. This was most likely because Saloonkeeper Earp was temporarily looking, not working. It was time to move on. Allie later commented:

> Two-three years at the most was all we could
> seem to stand in one place, we was that restless.
> Virge used to say, "Well, Allie, after a while all
> we'll have to do is put out the fire and call the
> dog."
> Yep, that's the way it was. Virge was a desert
> rat. I was only a desert mouse.[26]

Virgil Earp had decided to throw in with a new booming mining camp, north of San Bernardino, near the Nevada line.

FOOTNOTES

1. Waters, *Earp Brothers*, p. 207.
2. There is an extensive file of Earp-related material in the Colton Public Library; many of the pieces are photocopies of important documents from other collections.
3. An ad for Nick's Gem Saloon appeared for the first time in the Colton *Semi-Tropic* on November 27, 1880.
4. Two good newspaper summaries of Colton's past are in the Los Angeles *Evening Express*, January 21, 1889, and Colton *Courier*, October 30, 1922. See also Clark Harding Jones, "A History of the Development and Progress of Colton, California, 1873-1900," M.A. Thesis, Claremont Graduate School, 1951, copy in Colton Public Library.
5. See "Report of Mission Agency, August 20, 1888," in *Report of the Secretary of the Interior* (Washington, Vol. 2, 1888), pp. 10-20, for an understanding of how Colton fit into the administrative arrangement.
6. Some of this 1884 data is from Fred Holladay, "The Earp Clan in San Bernardino County," *Heritage Tales* [San Bernardino Historical Society], I (1978), 106. The San Bernardino *Daily Times* of August 20, 1884, contains the full proceedings of the Republican Convention, including the names of all candidates, and names of those who were merely "possibles."
7. *Arizona Daily Star*, July 6, 1886.
8. Waters, *Earp Brothers*, pp. 213-14.
9. Los Angeles *Times*, July 3, 1886; Holladay, "Earp Clan," p. 106.
10. San Bernardino *Weekly Times*, May 21, 1887; the arresting officer had been Virgil Earp.
11. Adelia Earp Edwards Memoirs, Colton Public Library.

12. San Bernardino *Daily Times*, July 14, 1887.
13. Ibid., July 20, 1887; Los Angeles *Evening Express*, July 20, 1887.
14. San Bernardino *Daily Times*, August 26, 1887.
15. Jones, "History of Colton" thesis, contains extracts of most Colton laws, and is a good history of the evolution of city government.
16. Alford E. Turner and Wm. W. Oster compiled notes of references to Virgil in the city council minutes and have deposited typescripts in the Earp file, Colton Public Library.
17. Dodge, *Undercover Agent*, pp. 83-87. The *Tombstone Epitaph* of August 20, 1887, on p. 3 had a variety of articles about recent train robberies, as well as this brief blurb: "Virgil Earp, city marshal of Colton, Cal., was in Fairbank last Sunday, looking for train robbers." Fairbank was a small settlement a few miles west of Tombstone.
18. The Phin Clanton incident is mentioned in the Stuart Lake-Wyatt Earp interview notes, Lake Papers, Huntington Library.
19. Turner-Oster Notes, Colton Public Library.
20. San Bernardino *Daily Courier*, June 28, 1889.
21. Ibid., December 26, 1889.
22. Holladay, "The Earp Clan," p. 12.
23. Allison comments in San Bernardino *Sun-Telegram*, April 17, 1957.
24. Pension file, 693-426, National Archives. Detailed descriptions of Virgil's wounds are given, as well as neighbor's affidavits, physician's report, and attorney's comments. He felt that his back wound caused his stomach problems.
25. Ibid. There is only one mention of Virgil in the *Tribune*, but all issues of September are heavy with comment on the

races at Santa Maria and San Luis Obispo. An article of September 25, "Voices of the Night," mentioned the many visitors in town, the "whir of the wheel and the rattle of the dice ringing out," all music to Virgil's ears, and most likely the inspiration for his presence in San Luis Obispo.

26. Waters, *Earp Brothers*, p. 215.

VIII: VANDERBILT
BONANZA QUEST

On January 25, 1891, a Piute Indian prospector named Bob Black found some interesting rock in the New York Mountains, several miles northwest of Needles, California. Assays determined that the rock contained paying gold, with bits of silver and other useful metals. By summer, a dozen or so men were on the site, and from that time on J. P. Taggart and J. H. Patton would be the dominant figures in that mining camp.[1]

The name Vanderbilt was given to this barren ground by early miners, who hoped that the camp's future would be associated with wealth and influence similar to that of the namesake. In one of the greater ironies of place-name bestowing, the town of Vanderbilt, with not a drop of water in sight, was named after a family that had earned its fortune in shipping.

The region of the discovery was at an elevation of 4,500 feet above sea level, and in a single year could have temperature varying from 120 to 30 degrees. Five inches of rainfall would be

187

considered a wetter than normal year. In fact, throughout most of its career as a mining settlement, Vanderbilt had to bring in water by wagon from Needles.

This was a hard rock camp, meaning that the paying gold was found in quartz veins, in this instance in company with granite deposits. There was no placer gold here, no bits of dust and nuggets to be sought by the individual prospector or miner. Hard rock mining meant hard work, mills, engines, and all sorts of heavy equipment in order to mine and crush the quartz. From the beginning, then, Vanderbilt was a mining camp of large investors capable of attracting new money to buy machinery.[2]

Vanderbilt was in the northeastern part of San Bernardino County, not far from the Arizona and Nevada lines. There was no railway within fifty miles of the place, and in a hard rock camp this could not be tolerated. For a camp to prosper, it was essential to have a rail system, to transport the boilers, crushers, and other equipment, as well as shipments of concentrated ore and provisions. Denver capitalist Isaac E. Blake became interested in the potential of the Vanderbilt region and arranged the financing of a rail system. By the end of 1893, the Nevada Southern had built a line as far as Manvel. From there it was only a four-mile carriage run to Vanderbilt.[3]

By late 1893 the word had gotten out, and the Vanderbilt boom was on. The leading early mines were the Vanderbilt, Gold Bronze, Gold Bar, Stanley, Crystal, Queen of the Night, Bonanza King, Boomerang, and others of similar exotic and enthusiastic names. Big machinery was in place, and at the Gold Bronze there were six shafts working for ore. The camp was "bustling and lively."

By January of 1893, there were about 500 people in the vicinity, with 150 residing in Vanderbilt. There were fifty tents, two stores, a saloon, and three restaurants, as well as a thrice-

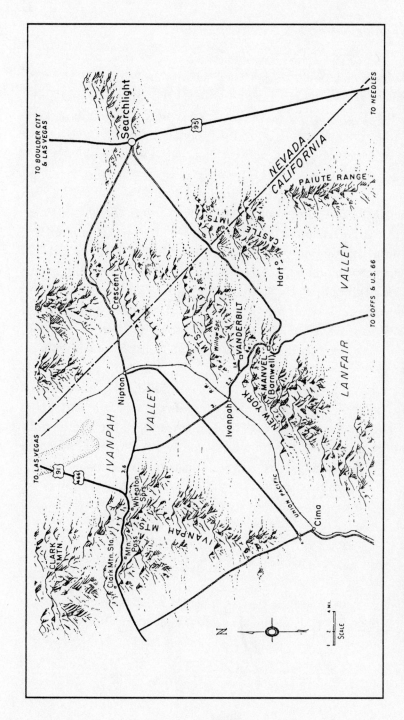

Virgil's path to the new mining camp of Vanderbilt in 1894 took him to the middle of nowhere, in one of the most rugged, hot places in California. Desert Magazine, July, 1957

weekly stage. A post office was established in February. The new community also had a bordello, with the madame in charge known as Diamond Tooth Lil, or Death Valley Diane. Young Fred Williams arrived there around this time and later recalled: "I saw nobody armed and all were well disposed and sociable."[4]

Such goings-on in a new mining camp, located in the same county, must have excited Virgil Earp, if not Allie. The San Bernardino *Times-Index* of April 28, 1893, announced that Virgil Earp had arrived in Vanderbilt with a wagon load of lumber and gambling equipment. The quiet, routine life of Colton and San Bernardino would be placed in the past. The Earp wanderlust and the call of the green cloth were stirring in Virgil again.

In the next few months there were sounds of hammering and sawing, and the result was Vanderbilt's only two-story building, which was promptly dubbed "Earp's Hall," although some locals referred to it as the Whist Club Saloon. This became the town social center, containing a saloon, dance hall, and gaming tables. It was even used occasionally for church services and court proceedings. Earp's Hall had another attraction, the presence of Virgil Earp. A well known figure in the West, he was a congenial saloon keeper, and had a reputation for strength and no-nonsense. The idea of combining church services with a gambling hall is the sort of thing that only someone of Virgil's reputation could arrange.

By this time, the *Needles Eye* carried a regular column of Vanderbilt news. The issue of November 4, 1893, reported:

> There was a dance at Erp's hall this week.
> Everybody was there, and it exceeded all past
> events.

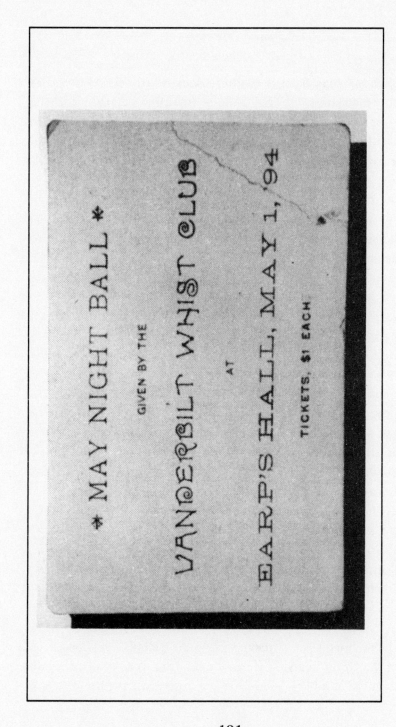

Everybody may have been there because there was no other place for everybody to go. Allie's memoirs are thin for the Vanderbilt years, and she most likely did not have much to do in this masculine environment. To placate her, Virgil erected one of the few rock-built houses in town, located about a hundred yards above the Gold Bronze Mine, near the bottom of a hill.

Faro, church services, and speeches were not all that concerned Virgil Earp. He was ever the fight promoter, and he arranged several boxing contests in the hall. One in particular, in mid-August of 1893, received a full column in the *Needles Eye*. The bout involved John Lee, "a colored man," the champion of northern Arizona, and Hank Lorraine, a "well known athlete on the coast." Virgil had constructed a twenty-foot ring in a corner of the hall, and more than 100 paying customers were on hand for the match.

Virgil was the referee, and Dr. James P. Booth of Needles, the time-keeper. The men gave a good fight for the entire ten rounds, and in the last round Lorraine pulverized Lee so badly that he "failed to respond at the call." Lorraine had a "shower bath" after the fight and mixed with the joyous crowd.

This was Vanderbilt's height of bonanza, and Virgil, too, felt that he was part of a rich, permanent camp. The *Needles Eye* of October 9, 1894, reported:

> Virg Earp is remodeling the inside of his saloon
> and says he will soon have a metropolitan estab-
> lishment. He has also put on an addition to the
> rear.

In 1894, Virgil was interviewed and officially registered as a voter in the Great Register of San Bernardino County. The details recorded give us a very good physical description of him. He was six feet one inch tall, of light complexion, light brown hair, and blue-gray eyes. He had been born in Kentucky, and was a merchant now residing in Vanderbilt. Under the category marks or scars, the entry read: "left arm crippled."

Some of the best information on the operation of Earp's Hall comes from J. O. Fisk, who as a young man lived in Vanderbilt, worked in the mines as a hoist tender, and was a frequent visitor to the Earp establishment. He claimed that Virgil's crippled arm did not interfere with his serving of drinks, nor with his ability to take care of troublemakers, "as more than one found out when tossed through the swinging doors to land on the cactus beds outside." Virgil was also adept at handling gambling cards, although for this he relied mostly on two "sharpers," known as High Pockets and Blood Alley Mose. For musical entertainment, Virgil had hired a fiddler and a reed organ player, known as the "orchestra."[6]

Fisk was present one night when a drunken miner created a disturbance when the Whist Club was holding a dance on the second floor. The drunk was locked in an empty power shaft which served as a makeshift jail, but escaped, went back to the dance, and shot up the organ:

> His life wouldn't have been worth much but it was discovered the organ would still play so on the promise of good behavior the miner was not bothered.

According to Fisk, who was nineteen during his Vanderbilt days, Virgil was a cheerful, agreeable man, "kind of studious," and always took part in the dances and get-togethers. "He was a pretty nice, gentlemanly sort of fellow, I liked him very much."[7]

Fisk had fond but realistic memories of the rough life at Vanderbilt:

> There was no plumbing and not a single bath
> tub in the entire district; we used the good old
> wash tub instead. Drinking water was hauled in by
> the barrel and sold at high prices. Fuel, packed for
> miles by burro trains, was expensive. That did not
> matter so much in summer when temperatures
> stood well over the century mark, but sometimes
> winter months brought snow and icy winds that
> kept those wood-trains working overtime.[8]

Virgil decided to test his popularity with his fellow citizens, and at the same time get into what he did best, being a lawman. He put his name in as candidate for constable of Needles Township. Naturally, he ran as a Republican. Because Needles and Vanderbilt were in the same township, and because two constables were allotted per township, it was agreed before the election that Needles and Vanderbilt would receive one each.

Earp's Hall was designated as the polling place in Vanderbilt.

In spite of Virgil's popularity, and in spite of having the voting take place in Earp's Hall, Virgil Earp lost the election. The results:

Keyes, Democrat & Republican	166
Hamerstadt, Independent	121
Earp, Republican	26
McNail, Democrat	15

The above represents just the Vanderbilt polling, but the township-wide tally was just as bad for Virgil. Even with the Needles total included, his vote numbered only 84. He had not been able to convert his popularity into victory over the more established locals, F. R. Keyes and A. Hamerstadt. Virgil's problem was that Vanderbilt was a heavily Democratic camp. For example, when the Democratic Committee came to Vanderbilt to register voters, they anticipated between sixty and seventy; more than 150 registered. Virgil was a loyal Republican, so continued party loyalty meant a crushing defeat.[9]

When the election was over, Virgil had to file a campaign expense claim with the county, and the total came to $22.00. Among the costs were $1.00 for stage fare to Manvel; $2.50, rail fare, Blake to Manvel; $3.00, printing of posters in Needles; $6.40, for "segars and Meals on the trip."[10]

Most precious metals camps have a short life, and Vanderbilt was no exception. Although mining would continue for decades, the years 1893-94 were the bonanza period, after which there was a rapid tailing off. Virgil, as well as others, saw this. Even by the end of 1894, it was clear that Vanderbilt had no future. A special Vanderbilt School District had been created in 1894, and by the end of the year at least 100 men were employed in Vanderbilt mines earning about $3.00 a day. But schools, and number of men employed, are not the factors which decide the future of a mining camp. When the good ore runs out, the communities fold.

More and more ominous signs were appearing. In July of 1894, merchant S. F. Holcomb, declaring that business was dull, moved his operation back to Needles. In August, the new local newspaper, the *Vanderbilt Shaft*, suspended publication.

The December 27, 1894, issue of the *Needles Eye* carried several items about Vanderbilt. The "S. M. S." held an entertainment in Earp's Hall, and a dance was given following the program. A grand ball was to be held in Earp's Hall Christmas Eve. And a third story:

195

> Virgil Earp has sold his building, comprising
> saloon, public hall and dwelling, to Brown and
> Thompson, presumably for Charley Smithson.

Shortly after the beginning of the New Year, Virgil and Allie Earp went back to their home in Colton, where they spent the winter months planning their next foray. By this time, Wyatt had sold his San Diego property and was spending some time in Colorado. Wyatt and Virgil exchanged letters, and the news of the success at the mining camp in Cripple Creek, Colorado, started both brothers thinking about bonanza again—not so much about picks and shovels and shafts and hoists, but about the type of bonanza that thrilled both of them. They would go to Cripple Creek and open a saloon.

FOOTNOTES

1. A good discovery account is in *Needles Eye*, April 22, 1893.
2. Interesting Vanderbilt summaries are in Los Angeles *Evening Express*, November 10, 1893, and Alan Hensher and Larry Vredenburgh, *Ghost Towns of the Upper Mojave Desert* (Los Angeles, 1987), pp. 82-90.
3. The *Needles Eye* carried regular reports on railroad construction.
4. Hensher, *Ghost Towns*, p. 82.
5. *Needles Eye*, August 18, 1894.
6. O. J. Fisk, "Treasures from Vanderbilt," *Westways*, June, 1952, pp. 22-23.
7. Fisk, interview notes, San Bernardino *Sun-Telegram*, April 17, 1957.
8. Fisk, *Westways*, p. 23.
9. Virgil's run for constable can be followed in the *Needles Eye*, October 23, 30, November 6, 1894.
10. Fred Holladay, "As Rich as Vanderbilt," *Heritage Tales* [San Bernardino Historical Society], II (1979), 10. Nell Murbarger, who has explored much of the California desert terrain, wrote an interesting article about Vanderbilt and its remains: "The Deserted New Yorks," *True West*, January/February, 1965, pp. 12-15, 68-69.

IX: REST, BONANZA, AND DEATH

The Earp brothers' stay in Cripple Creek left no great imprint in the local press, or on historians. This Colorado gold camp had gotten off to a quick start in 1890-91 and by 1893 was in full swing with saloons, laundries, merchant houses, hotels, and barber shops, all hastily erected to take care of the burgeoning mining population. Virgil and Wyatt Earp, their wives, and a few other relatives and friends arrived in Cripple Creek in the summer of 1895.

There was a lot going on in Cripple Creek, and much money to be made. But saloon keeping and running a gambling hall were activities one did at the beginning of a boom, not in the middle. The investors, doers, and chance-takers had beaten the Earp brothers to the site and were well established by the time Virgil and Wyatt arrived. Timing was everything, and they missed it. Earlier at Vanderbilt Virgil had followed an ideal timetable for a new mining camp: arrive early and leave before it's too late. Wyatt would later do the same in the Nome gold fields. But Cripple Creek

199

was not for the Earps. In Wyatt's many letters there is no reference to Cripple Creek, and his biographer Stuart Lake does not even mention the few months there. The Earps would go elsewhere to find excitement.

For Virgil and Allie Earp Prescott, Arizona, was the choice. Virgil had spent many months there in the late 1860s, and the couple had lived there from 1877 to 1879. They had fond memories, and Allie in particular longed for the place. The Arizona *Journal-Miner* of October 23, 1895 reported:

> Virgil Earp, an old time resident of Prescott, and one of the historical characters of the territory, arrived here last evening with a view of locating here again. He came direct from Cripple Creek, Colorado. Mr. Earp will be remembered by all old timers in Prescott for the part he took, as a deputy sheriff under Ed Bowers, in the fight which took place south of town in which two cowboys were killed. In later years Mr. Earp and his brothers figured prominently as officers at Tombstone in ridding that community of outlaws.

The same issue mentioned that Virgil had rented a house in Prescott and expected his family in a day or so. The word "family" probably referred to Allie's niece, a daughter of her sister Lydia, and her husband. They would live with the Virgil Earp family for several years. The news about Virgil's arrival was picked up by newspapers in Phoenix, Tucson, and Tombstone.

In the same column appeared a few lines that to most readers were unrelated, but which most likely made Virgil smile. The Nevada Southern Railroad, which had been scheduled to go into

Prescott, Arizona, Gurley Street. Sharlot Hall Museum

Vanderbilt, was sold at sheriff's auction in San Bernardino. Virgil had planned his departure perfectly.

In 1895 Prescott was a community of 4,500 inhabitants, slightly larger than when the Earps had lived there previously. There was still considerable mining activity around Prescott, and the region was becoming well known for stock raising. The political situation, though, had altered. In 1889 the state capital had been shifted from Prescott to Phoenix. Yet, Prescott was still the center of a large agricultural and mining region, and had a fair share of political and governmental business as the seat of Yavapai County.

The new mining activity claimed Virgil's interest. There were half a dozen producing gold mines, with large machinery in place, many promising prospects, and some decent producers of silver, copper, and lead. The *Engineering & Mining Journal* in its report covering 1896 claimed that Yavapai County "is able to give a good account of itself." Most of the excitement and profits, though, were from the Congress Mine in the southern part of the county. Yet, there were more prospectors and investors looking at properties than at any time in the past. All kinds of gold mining were under way, or under consideration: placer mining, including hydraulic operations; quartz, or hard rock mining; and all sorts of mills, crushing machines, and other marks of big time mining activity were visible. Unlike in the earlier period, Prescott was now well served by rail lines, which aided greatly in the transporting of ore and large machinery.

Another indication of the high interest in mining was the growth in business done by Prescott merchants. On some days, dozens of burros and large wagons, all heavily laden, could be seen leaving the back loading alleys, headed with provisions for the several hundred mining camps scattered in the mountains, in all directions from Prescott. By late spring of 1896, this enthusiasm

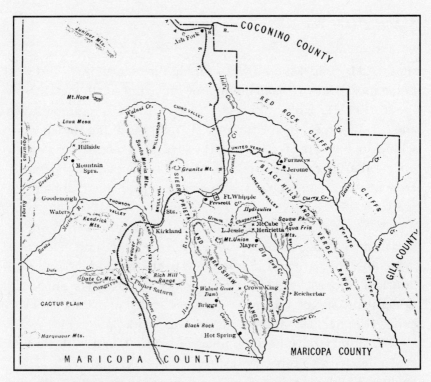

Portion of Yavapai County. Engineering & Mining Journal,
June 19, 1897

had led to the formation of the Prescott Mining Exchange, to
facilitate buying and selling of shares, and to promote prospecting,
mining, and milling.[1]

One of the territory's best known mining districts was the
Hassayampa, a few miles south and west of Prescott. There were
gold placer as well as hard rock operations there. Virgil became
attracted to the region, where he invested in a working proposition with W. H. Harlan. The mine, known as the Grizzly, was
owned by W. C. Hanson, who leased the property to Harlan and
Virgil.

With Harlan, Virgil linked up with one of the movers in the
Hassayampa District. Harlan had worked in half a dozen local

sites, and by mid-1896 he was running three small mills and was doing most of the custom milling for the many small operators in the district. Harlan's mills were between the Hassayampa River and Groom Creek. By the summer of 1896, Virgil and Harlan were taking ore out of the Grizzly Mine and working it nearby in a steam operated arrastra [rock crusher]. Harlan's practice was to have a crew of five or six on hand, so there were probably that many at work on the Grizzly.[2]

On November 17, 1896, while Virgil and Harlan were working in a tunnel going into the mine, there was a sudden cave-in "catching Mr. Earp and pinning him to the ground." Virgil was knocked unconscious for several hours. Dr. Charles Abbott, a druggist and surgeon from Prescott, was called in to look over the battered miner. Dr. Abbott himself was working several nearby claims, so may have been familiar with Virgil, and with Virgil's problems. Virgil's hip was dislocated, his feet and ankles were badly crushed, his head severely cut, and the rest of his body was a collection of serious bruises. Virgil's life was in peril, but this did not end his mining career.[3]

The *Journal-Miner* gave a progress report on January 23, 1897, mentioning that Virgil was recovering and could get around on crutches:

> Mr. Earp has had two or three experiences in
> his life which very few men would have lived
> through, this being one of them. He has been shot
> all to pieces, and crushed in this mine accident, but
> still has hopes as well as good prospects of living
> to a ripe old age.

The newspaper account may have been graphic, but was not exaggerated. Virgil had been seriously wounded in the Tombstone

204

shootout, then a few months later ambushed, leaving his left arm shattered. The mine accident left few parts of his body intact.

After spending further months in recovery, Virgil and Allie moved out to the Kirkland Valley, some miles to the west and south of Prescott. For the next few years, Virgil filled the role of Arizona rancher, although because of his health, and only modest finances, he was not an important figure locally in that sphere. He had some horses and cattle, and even had a few hands on the payroll. He was treated like a local sage. The *Journal-Miner* in the spring of 1897 quoted Virgil Earp, "a well known Arizonan," on the weather for the coming summer. In October of 1899, Captain A. F. Banta, the prominent Arizona journalist, stopped in to see Virgil, commented on his cattle business, and gave a report on the Earp family; Virgil had just heard from Wyatt, who was doing well in the Alaskan gold fields. Naturally, Banta reported that Wyatt had "taken out $50,000 in gold," hinting the gold was from the mines. Wyatt, instead, had mined the miners who patronized his Dexter Saloon in Nome.[4]

Virgil's time in the late 1890s seems to have been split among small-time ranching, visiting, and, against most logic, working in the shaft of the Grizzly again. One report from the summer of 1897 described Virgil as "experting a mining claim with money and muscle."[5] At the end of each autumn, Virgil and Allie packed up, left the beautiful Kirkland Valley, and headed to Prescott to spend the winter. One newspaper account from late 1898 followed his moves and also helped explain why Virgil was so well liked in the region:

> Mr. and Mrs. V. W. Earp have moved in from Kirkland Valley to spend the winter in Prescott. Mr. Earp has lived and traveled all over the west and says there is no country equal to Arizona.[6]

What does one do while wintering in Prescott? In Virgil Earp's case, one did what one liked and did best. Virgil often served as special officer, or deputy, for the local courts and law enforcement agencies.

One particularly nasty case in November of 1898 had Virgil running between Prescott and Jerome, and facing arrest himself. Three Jerome editors, James and Claude Thompson and a reporter named Lawrence, were being sued for libel, related to political campaign writing and the pros and cons of the management of the copper mining firms in Jerome. An arrest warrant was sworn in Justice Moore's court by John Burns, one of those afflicted by the Jerome journalists' writings:

> Mr. Moore appointed Virgil Earp a special constable and Mr. Earp hied him over the taxless to Jerome with his warrant. He nabbed Lawrence and James Thompson and brought them in last evening.

The fellows were jailed, paid bail, and were released the next day. This did not end the matter. Virgil was arrested that same night, charged with false imprisonment.

The episode, almost comic in its cell-changing, was based on faulty understanding of Virgil's authority. The "false imprisonment" charge was leveled because it was not known by all parties that Virgil Earp in this matter was Constable Earp, acting in accord with Justice Moore's court. Needless to say, Virgil did not spend any time in jail.[7]

In the fall of 1898, Virgil received a letter from a lady in Portland, Oregon. Was he the Virgil Earp who in 1860 had married Ellen Rysdam? If so, the writer was Earp's daughter Janie. The account thrilled Virgil and Allie. As Allie recalled:

> There! All these years and me and Virge never
> had a baby, and here was Virge findin' out for the
> first time in his life he had a grown-up young lady
> daughter, Jane![8]

After the Civil War, when Ellen and her family moved West, she believing that he had been killed, Virgil decided not to pursue the matter further: he "philosophically decided that the best thing he could do was to keep out of her way." Ellen had married Robert Eaton in Washington Territory, and they eventually settled in Oregon. Ellen, Virgil's child bride, was also yet alive, and a widow. Apparently over the years she had shared some memories with her daughter of Iowa and her long lost father, Virgil Earp. Janie, now in her late thirties, and the wife of Levi Law, kept seeing reference in the newspapers to this fellow from Tombstone and Prescott, a famous lawman named Virgil Earp. She wrote the introductory letter, setting off a chain of events unusual in any family.[9]

Virgil replied at once in a letter "filled to the brim with questions as to where she was born and what was the name of her mother, was her mother alive and where did she live." Janie replied with the correct answers to all of Virgil's questions, and in a day or so she received a telegram from Virgil. "He was her father and would be up to see her as soon as he could manage, which was very soon."

Winter and the illness of Jane interfered with a quick reunion. Early in 1899 Virgil learned that Janie was seriously ill with pneumonia. No longer hesitating, Virgil and Allie Earp went to Portland, stepped off the train, and met his daughter Jane and his ex-wife Ellen:

> It was a meeting of great feelings and after
> these had been dispensed with, they went to her

> home. There she [Jane] sat up late at night with her
> father and he would recall the happenings of his
> life after his entrance to serve in the Civil War.

The reunion and visiting lasted several days before Virgil and Allie headed back to Arizona. The unusual nature of the situation was covered by much of the Western press, with illustrations of Virgil and his long-lost wife and daughter. A new series of friendships and relationships was forged which would last even beyond Virgil's death.[10]

Politics and government service were prime interests of Nick, Virgil, and Wyatt Earp, and they frequently got involved in party organization, lobbying, elections, and appointments. All three of this unusual trio, served in more than twenty elected and appointed positions.

When Virgil moved back to Prescott in late 1895, he did not at once become active in Republican circles, deciding to re-establish himself further before making any noises. For example, the Yavapai County Republicans held a several-day meeting in September of 1896, and practically every Republican in the county was mentioned for some reason or another, but there is no listing of the name Virgil Earp.[11]

By 1900, though, the reinvigorated Virgil Earp threw himself into partisan politics. In September, the Republican county convention was held in Prescott over a several day span. Virgil attended as the delegate from Kirkland Valley. Early in the proceedings, a committee of five was appointed to oversee platform and resolutions; Virgil Earp was a member. As a further indication of Virgil's reputation for fair play, he and Arthur Gage were designated as the convention tellers whose job would be to keep the votes straight and above board.

When it was time for nominations to office, Judge E. W. Wells

Virgil, wife and daughter. Portland Oregonian, April 22, 1899

placed the name of Virgil Earp before the convention as the Republican candidate for sheriff of Yavapai County. "He was nominated by acclamation."[12] Judge Wells had known Virgil for years; the Earp sawmill provided the lumber for the Wells residence in 1879.

Time, wounds, maybe even the possibility of defeat—something weighed heavily on Virgil right after the convention. Within days, he withdrew as candidate for sheriff, and the party was left without a candidate for this vital position. The *Journal-Miner* quoted a Florence, Arizona, paper as saying that Earp, a man of reputation more or less good, had withdrawn. The *Journal-Miner* concluded:

> As Earp has refused to run, his reputation is
> more than less good.[13]

Virgil's withdrawal prompted ex-sheriff George Ruffner of Prescott to file as an Independent candidate. In the election in early November, the incumbent, J. L. Munds, was re-elected sheriff with 1527 votes to 1341 for Ruffner. In the other county-wide office races, the margin was greater for the victors, most of them Democrats. It may have been that Republican candidate Virgil Earp could have given Munds a closer contest than Ruffner had. In the several newspaper notices of Virgil's withdrawal, none mentioned the cause. The most reasonable conclusion is that he finally decided that the demands of being sheriff in a large county like Yavapai would be too much for his bullet-ridden, mine crushed body.

One incident from the September convention needs to be examined, a speech made by Virgil, because it represents the only known collection of exaggerations and braggadocio uttered by him. After his nomination, he made "one of the best speeches of the evening." He became the accomplished politician. He spun a career that had not existed. He made himself the leading law enforcement officer in Dodge City, the scourge of all outlaws in the West, and so forth. A few excerpts from that speech follow:

> In 1874 I went to Dodge City. . . .I had been there only a short time when business men and property owners came to me and said, "Earp, you must help us to overcome the lawlessness in this city;" I replied, "I don't want it, give it to someone else." They said, "If you don't take the city marshalship we will have to leave town." So in the interest of law and order I accepted.

Virgil went on in a similar vein, mentioning Prescott and Tombstone. In all cases, city fathers came to him, begging him to take office. He resisted, but finally yielded to the needs of a desperate citizenry.[14]

The reality had been far different. He sought office as constable in Prescott in 1878, and was elected. He ran for city marshal twice in Tombstone, but was defeated each time. His appointment to that position came when Marshal Ben Sippy skipped town. Dodge City historians will smile at his claims of city marshalship. There is no proof that Virgil Earp served so much as a day on the Dodge City police force. Also, city fathers had not always come begging for his help; in the new town of Vanderbilt, Virgil got only a handful of votes when he ran for constable in 1894.

Virgil Earp could have given an accurate description of his fascinating career in that speech. The shootout in the streets of Prescott in 1877, the famous shootout in Tombstone in 1881, his control over the lawless cowboys pestering Tombstone, would

211

have enthralled his audience. Instead, Virgil became typical politician, and enhanced his roles, exaggerated his reputation.

Perhaps he was learning from brother Wyatt. In many newspaper interviews, and in a series of articles in the San Francisco *Examiner* in 1896, Wyatt explained how authorities had begged him to go to troubled Tombstone, carrying a commission of deputy U. S. marshal. Wyatt had intentionally muddied the waters; Virgil, not Wyatt, had been the deputy U. S. marshal.

The sad fact is that both men had notable careers as Western lawmen, with no need to dress up their roles, yet both of them did so.

Another controversy involving the Earp family stems from the killing of Warren Earp on July 6, 1900. Warren, who had a history of drinking and fighting, had been employed as a rancher for several years near Willcox, Cochise County. In Brown's Saloon, he got into an argument with John Boyett; he accused Boyett of wanting to kill him. Warren challenged him, Boyett went to get a gun, came back, and as Warren advanced towards him, Boyett shot him in the heart. As it turned out, Warren Earp was not armed. The coroner's inquest, held on July 6, cleared Boyett of any wrong-doing, stating that witnesses agreed that Warren had pushed Boyett into the deadly confrontation.

There is very little to add to the above incident. The problem is that many writers *have* added, without much to back their wild speculations. One scenario has Wyatt coming down from Alaska, joining up with brother Virgil, then going to Cochise County to avenge brother Warren. Wyatt never left Alaska that summer, as recently unearthed court testimony and newspaper articles from Alaska establish. And, although there is one source that claims Virgil killed Boyett, there is no evidence for such a killing—it is not even certain when or how Boyett met his death.[15]

The Virgil Earp property at the turn of the century was in the

Kirkland Valley, and not far from Skull Valley. In fact, in the many newspaper references to the Earps, both valleys were mentioned from time to time. On March 6, 1900, V. W. Earp filed a homestead exemption claim in the land office in Prescott, for parcels in Sections 17 and 20 of Township 12. He had Kirkland residents Rudy, Earnhart, More, and Langley attest to his residence and cultivation of the land there.

Although Prescott, and the Kirkland Valley, may have been the ideal of what a community should be for Virgil and Allie, that did not mean they would stay there. Virgil was ever the looker and wanderer. After the winter of 1900-1901, which they spent quietly in Prescott, they passed more time elsewhere, especially in California. In 1901, Virgil and Wyatt applied for a gambling hall permit in the city of Colton, but they were turned down. Colton had never been a wide-open town, and Justice Earp had been retired for some years, taking away the little influence the Earps had left in that community.

By late 1901, Nick Earp had fallen on hard times. He had remarried in 1893, and had become very active in San Bernardino pioneer activities for a few years, but his health began to deteriorate. In 1901 he was placed in the Veterans Home in Sawtelle, on the western border of Los Angeles. In 1902 and 1903, Virgil and Allie spent weeks visiting Nick at the Veterans home, probably staying with brother James Earp, who had moved to nearby Santa Monica to be near his father.[16]

Virgil began to close out his Arizona affairs, selling off some property and animals in 1902 and 1903. He was listed in the Yavapai County Great Register in 1902, but does not appear in the 1904 listing. He was seeking a further excitement.

In late 1901, Wyatt Earp returned from Alaska, where he had had a successful two years as operator of a saloon in Nome. Wyatt, too, was looking for another frontier, and after a few months in

213

Land claim notice. Sharlot Hall Museum

Los Angeles he headed for the latest bonanza, the strikes at
Tonopah, Nevada. Wyatt and Josie spent much of 1902 in
Tonopah, where he set up the Northern Saloon and did some
prospecting. He also served briefly as a deputy U. S. marshal, with
authority in Nye County. After a leisurely prospecting journey
through the Nevada and California deserts, Wyatt and Josie
headed back to San Bernardino and Los Angeles.[17]

Sometime in 1903 or 1904, an Earp family gathering occurred
in San Bernardino, and even elderly, infirm Nick Earp was brought
in for the occasion. Virgil, Wyatt, James, and Adelia were on hand,
with their spouses and children. The new strike at Goldfield, a few
miles south of Tonopah, was the hot topic of discussion, and Virgil
and Wyatt were planning to investigate the opportunities. Impor-

214

tant gold finds had been located there in 1902 by men bankrolled by Jim Butler, who had discovered the fabulous Tonopah deposits. Adelia described how Virgil and Wyatt looked as they sat together on the large green ottoman and "stretched those long legs along that thick green carpet." According to Adelia:

> Virgil said to me, booming like he did all of a sudden, "Deelie pour some coffee now, and put some of that there whiskey in." We all had a real fine time.[18]

The news about Goldfield came in increasing flashes of enthusiasm, as the Goldfield District was organized on October 20, 1903, and the new Town of Goldfield was laid out within a week. Virgil and Allie decided to throw in with the excitement. They had taken care of their Arizona holdings, but decided to keep their Colton home. In mid-1904, the Virgil Earps headed for the bonanza camp of Goldfield.

There was no place in Goldfield for Virgil Earp, the miner, and Virgil Earp, the saloon man, did not have the capital to invest in what was turning out to be a major Western mining center. Big money was in town, and Virgil could not start a bucket shop and hope to prosper.

A man of Virgil's background and personality did not long remain out of work. On January 26, 1905, Virgil was sworn in as deputy sheriff of Esmeralda County by Sheriff J. F. Bradley, with the specific assignment of working in Goldfield. The terms of Bradley's appointment were "during my pleasure." Bradley was also ex-officio assessor for the county, but assessor's duties were stricken from the page of Virgil's Oath of Office.[19]

In addition to his position as deputy sheriff, Virgil was also designated Special Officer, to serve in the National Club, one of

215

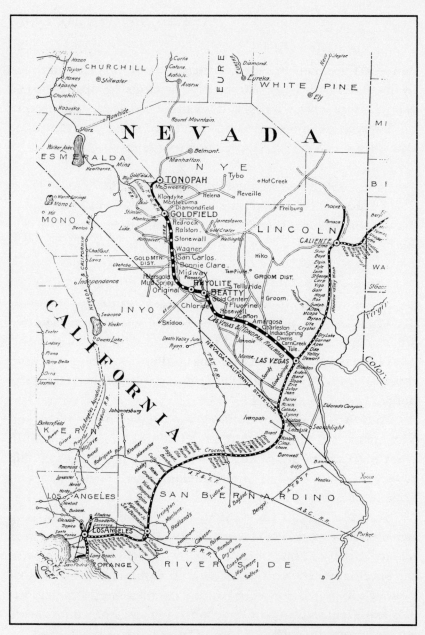

Wyatt tried the mining camp of Tonopah in 1902, and Virgil's last stop was in Goldfield, where he died in 1905. Natural History Museum, Los Angeles

the more important watering spots in the booming mining town. In other words, Virgil Earp, the feared city marshal of Tombstone, was acting as a bouncer in a mining camp saloon.

The *Tonopah Sun* of February 5, 1905, reported on Virgil's new position:

> Verge Earp, a brother of Wyatt and one of the famous family of gunologists, is acting as deputy sheriff in the National Club, Goldfield. Verge is a mild looking individual and to outward view presents none of the characteristics that have made the family name a familiar one in the west and in all the bonanza camps of the country from Mexico to Alaska.

The *Sun* also mentioned that Wyatt was expected any day, and that the brothers also owned a few mining claims near Bullfrog "out of which they hope to make a goodly sum."

Goldfield had also attracted Tex Rickard, who had made a fortune out of saloon keeping in Nome, and who had known Wyatt in that Alaskan city. Tex arrived in Goldfield early in the game and in January of 1905 opened his "Northern," which became one of the most famous saloons in the history of the frontier. Carousing miners could go into the Northern, hear some bombast and great tales from Tex Rickard, then go next door and have a drink with Virgil Earp.

Goldfield, a large camp, was not a particularly violent one. Sheriff Bradley had a collection of nightwatchmen, under-sheriffs, and deputies. Although Virgil was a deputy sheriff, the position seems to have been especially created to give him a cloak of authority at the National Club. Deputy Al Jones was Sheriff Bradley's main local deputy. Aside from these county law enforce-

217

Goldfield, Nevada, was in its mining boom phase when Virgil Earp arrived early in 1905; he died there later in the year. Natural History Museum, Los Angeles

ment officers, the City of Goldfield also had constables, deputy constables, and nightwatchmen, all of whom were responsible to the city council.[20]

Virgil Earp figured in neither the court cases nor in the many incidents detailed in the Goldfield newspapers about thefts, assaults, or shootings. He became very sick with pneumonia, recovered, and had several relapses during his stay in Goldfield. He was bed-ridden much of the time. When he was at his post at the National Club, though, it is unlikely that anyone pestered him, or that he was unable to dispense his version of law and order. He was still a large man, and although one-armed, capable of drawing a pistol and buffaloing the malcontent.

In May of 1905 there was a scrape in the National, which started as a fist fight between John Redmond and Andy McGuinn over a gambling loss. Redmond lost, pulled a pistol and fired, hitting a bystander. Among the many accounts, there is no mention of Virgil Earp. He was most likely home in bed.[21]

Virgil's health deteriorated, and he was finally sent to the hospital next to the Miners' Union Hall in Goldfield. This was not the first time that Allie had seen her husband prone, gasping for life. She recalled:

> He said to me, "get me a cigar." Believing he was feeling better I did so. "Now," he said, "put Hickie's [his grand-niece] last letter under my pillow, light my cigar, and stay here and hold my hand.[22]

Virgil Earp died on October 19, 1905, of a pneumonia epidemic that swept Goldfield, claiming ten other lives in that same month.

220

OATH OF OFFICE.

STATE OF NEVADA,
County of Esmeralda \ ss

V. W. Earp do solemnly swear that I will support protect and defend the Constitution and Government of the United States and the Constitution and Government of the State of Nevada, against all enemies, whether domestic or foreign, and that I will bear true faith, allegiance and loyalty to the same, any ordinance or law of any State convention or Legislature to the contrary notwithstanding and further that I do this with a full determination, pledge and purpose, without any mental reservation or evasion whatsoever. And I do further solemnly swear that I have not fought a duel, nor sent nor accepted a challenge to fight a duel, nor been a second to either party, nor in any manner aided or assisted in such duel, nor been knowingly the bearer of such challenge or acceptance, since the adoption of the Constitution of the State of Nevada, and that I will not be so engaged or concerned directly or indirectly, in or about any such duel during my continuance in office. And further that I will well and faithfully perform all the duties of the office of _Deputy Sheriff_ on which I am about to enter so help me God.

Subscribed and sworn to before me this _27th_ day of _January_, 190_5_

_Louis ...
Notary Public_

Virgil W. Earp

Hawthorne, Nev. _Jan 26th_ 1905

I hereby designate and appoint _V. W. Earp_ of _Goldfield_ Deputy Sheriff and ex-officio Assessor in and for Esmeralda county, State of Nevada. _during my pleasure_

J. F. Bradley
Sheriff and ex-officio Assessor Esmeralda county, Nevada.

Virgil's last peace officer role. Nevada Historical Society

Virgil by this time was less widely known than younger brother Wyatt, and his obituaries were pretty much limited to newspapers in Arizona and Nevada. They stated the obvious, pointing out his long lawman career, the various towns where he lived, and his relationships with his brothers, Doc Holliday, Bat Masterson, and so forth. Naturally, there was a brief summary of the Tombstone shootout in most of the obituaries.[23]

Allie saw that Virgil's remains were shipped to Portland, Oregon, at the request of Virgil's daughter, Jane. Virgil Earp was buried in Riverview Cemetery in Portland, in a setting far removed in distance and atmosphere from the forested hills of Prescott, the noisy streets of Tombstone, or the gambling halls of Goldfield.[24]

FOOTNOTES

1. For mining near Prescott during this era, see *Engineering & Mining Journal*, February 27, 1897, and June 19, 1897; see also a detailed lisiting of most mining operations in *Arizona Weekly Journal-Miner*, January 1, 1896. For specific details of the Hassayampa, see the *Journal-Miner*, May 30, 1894.
2. Harlan's many operations are listed in the *Journal-Miner*, October 16, 1895, January 27, December 16, 1896.
3. *Journal-Miner*, November 18, 1896. There are several additional clippings regarding the cave-in and Virgil's recovery in the Archives, Sharlot Hall Museum, Prescott.
4. Virgil as weatherman, undated clipping, Archives, Sharlot Hall Museum; Banta interview, *Journal-Miner*, October 9, 1899.
5. *Pioche Record* (Nevada), August 26, 1897.
6. *Journal-Miner*, October 25, 29, 1898.
7. Series of clippings, Archives, Sharlot Hall Museum.
8. Waters, *Earp Brothers*, p. 215.
9. Portland *Oregonian*, April 22, 1899.
10. Turner, *Earps Talk*, pp. 106-108, for marriage details and Oregon history of the family, by relative George Bertrand.
11. The 1896 convention is well covered in the *Journal-Miner* of September 16.
12. Ibid., September 22, 26, 1900.
13. Clipping, Archives, Sharlot Hall Museum.
14. The speech is reprinted in Turner, *Earps Talk*, pp. 80-81.
15. The inquest, held July 6, 1900, is in the Superior Court files of Cochise County. There are interesting clipping files on Warren in the Colton Public Library and in the Sharlot Hall Museum. For the theory of Virgil being the avenger, see

222

Glenn Boyer, *I Married Wyatt Earp: The Recollections of Josephine Sarah Marcus Earp* (Tucson, 1976), pp. 203-204.

16. Several clippings in the Archives, Sharlot Hall Museum, indicate that Virgil was to visit Sawtelle. Nick would eventually die there on February 12, 1907; Los Angeles *Times*, February 14, 1907, II, 6. Virgil's brothers Newton and James also lived at the Veterans Home, or in Sawtelle, for a few years; both had seen Civil War service.

17. Some of this Nevada information is drawn from Jeffrey M. Kintop and Guy Louis Rocha, *The Earps' Last Frontier: Wyatt and Virgil Earp in the Nevada Mining Camps, 1902-1905* (Reno, 1990).

18. Adelia Earp Edwards Memoirs.

19. Virgil's Oath of Office; copy provided by Nevada Historical Society, Reno.

20. I have drawn most of these law and order comments from issues of the *Goldfield Review* and *Goldfield News*, bound volumes in the Huntington Library.

21. *Goldfield News*, May 26, 1905.

22. Holladay, "Earp Clan," p. 123.

23. A few obituaries: *Nevada State Journal*, October 25, 1905; *Tonopah Miner*, October 21, 1905; *Tombstone Prospector*, October 27, 1905; *Arizona Republican*, October 30, 1905.

24. Oregon newspaper clipping, August 8, 1958, contains an article about the burial, plus a photograph of Virgil's tombstone; copy in Colton Public Library.

AFTERWORD

Allie Earp, the loyal partner who had wandered the West with Virgil for thirty years, outlived him for another forty-two years. For a few years, Allie lived with Virgil's sister Adelia in San Bernardino. The two were more like sisters than sisters-in-law and remained intimate for several decades. Allie eventually moved into Los Angeles, but continued to visit San Bernardino and Colton a few times a year.[1]

Allie's closest companion during these Los Angeles years was her grand-niece, Mrs. C. E. [Hildreth] Halliwell, with whom she lived. Hildreth, the granddaughter of Allie's sister Lydia, had been born in Prescott at the home of Virgil and Allie and lived with them until she was six.

In Los Angeles, Hildreth was also in frequent contact with her Uncles James and Wyatt. James Earp was the first to pass on; he died in 1926, while staying with Hildreth. Wyatt died in Los Angeles early in 1929. Alvira Earp, known to friends and relatives as Allie, died in Los Angeles in Hildreth's home on November 14,

1947, and funeral services were held for her on November 17. Her ashes were placed on the grave of her sister-in-law Adelia Earp Edwards, her friend "Deelie," in the cemetery in San Bernardino.[2]

In the 1930s, Allie had met Frank Waters, a well known Western writer who became intrigued with her background.

He included some of the material in his book *The Colorado*, published in 1946 as part of the "Rivers of America" series. Waters interviewed Allie on many occasions, for hours on end.

When he finally put together a draft of some chapters, Allie had a chance to read the material, and she erupted. According to Hildreth Halliwell, "she [Allie] told him she would sue him" if he published the work. Hildreth spared no phrase in condemning the Waters efforts. Lies, treachery, exaggeration, and the like were what both Allie and Hildreth thought of Waters' prose.[3]

For reasons only Waters knew, he delayed publication of his work until 1960, when it appeared as *The Earp Brothers of Tombstone: The Story of Mrs. Virgil Earp*. Allie and Virgil Earp were served badly by Waters, who apparently had a singular mission: to tarnish the images of Wyatt and Virgil Earp.[4]

Some of the material in the Waters book is interesting, colorful, and accurate, especially regarding the private lives of Allie and Virgil. But Waters had a blind spot when it came to stating anything positive about the Earp brothers. He resented the myth that had emerged around Wyatt and felt it was his mission to give Wyatt, as well as his brothers, feet of clay.

Throughout the book, Waters placed heavy emphasis on the fact that the Earps were saloon men, gamblers. That meant, implied Waters, that they were no good. Waters had no feeling or knowledge of how important the saloon was on the frontier. In Dodge City, while serving as a police officer, Wyatt owned part of two saloons, and the Mayor, Jim "Dog" Kelly, had been put in office by the Saloon League. In Tombstone, Mayor Clum, the city councilmen, and leading mining executives could be found drinking, talking, and gaming in ten or more sporting houses. In Vanderbilt, in Earp's Hall, where drinks could be had, and faro played, the citizens had a meeting house, an election center, a music-theater site, and a general gathering place for the community, even for church services.

The examples could be continued, but the above is enough to indicate that to saloon-label a man in the American West in that era was not much of a condemnation. In the early phases of a boom camp, the saloon played an important social, economic, and political role, and it was not at all unusual for men of the law to be also men of the saloon; marshals, constables, sheriffs, and policemen frequently owned part or all of the drinking and gambling action in young Western mining towns.[5]

One chronicler of the Kansas cow towns explained the matter simply: the beef of the South was exchanged for the cash of the North. The city fathers of Wichita, Dodge City, and other cattle centers knew that financial prosperity meant getting the cattlemen's patronage. The cow towns did just that, by providing "gaming, drinking, and whoring."[6] The Tombstone situation was a bit different. In addition to the cattlemen from the surrounding countryside, the Tombstone merchants also provided the gaming, drinking, and whoring for the miners. In the Kansas cow towns, or in the mining settlement of Tombstone, the Earps, as well as hundreds of other enterprising businessmen, made a living by providing all that was expected in such a saloon environment. This was not, as Waters implied, a world of lawlessness. The Earps, in the Long Branch in Dodge, in the Oriental in Tombstone, and in the National Club in Goldfield, were businessmen and at the same time representatives of law and order.

It does appear, though, that Frank Waters had gotten some anti-Wyatt feeling and information from Allie. By the 1930s, when

227

the interviews took place, the myth of Wyatt Earp had become part of our heritage. Books, magazine and newspaper articles, and a few important movies had placed him in the upper rung in the pantheon of gunologists. Allie resented this, according to Hildreth Halliwell. Much of the important work in Tombstone had been Virgil's, and it was Virgil in Tombstone who was city chief of police and deputy U. S. marshal, two roles that Wyatt and his biographers "annexed" as the years passed. Allie may have felt that by unburdening herself to a writer like Waters, Virgil might get the recognition he deserved.[7]

The reputation of Virgil Earp need not rest on the rambling denunciations of Frank Waters, nor on the comments of any other writer. Virgil Earp received important appointments to office, and on several occasions he was elected by his fellow citizens to hold office. He was a prominent public figure wherever he lived, from 1877 until his death in 1905. Even when he died he was serving as a deputy sheriff. The public record, the oaths of office, the popular press, and the ballot box indicate that Virgil Earp's fellow citizens liked him as a person and trusted him with their lives and property.

The Tombstone years remain the highlight of his law enforcement career. That is why so much of the present book has been devoted to the situation there and in Cochise County, with the all-important rivalry between the Earps and the Clanton-McLaury-Behan crowd.

We should remember that in spite of all the Tombstone controversy, the city was a relatively safe place under the ironclad hand of City Marshal Virgil Earp.

On November 29, 1881, George Parsons in Tombstone made the following diary entry:

Fearful racket below [in Golden Eagle Brewery] all night with nearly a fight. A lie given. This is the hardest corner in town, 5th and Allen, and this building [Tribolet] I would be afraid of next rainy season. Shots fired once in awhile. Am wondering when a bullet will come through floor or wall.[8]

There were similar comments in the Parsons diary in the following days, such as "fights at both saloons" [Oriental and Golden Eagle].[9]

What Parsons knew, and what was evident to many citizens in Tombstone, was that Virgil Earp was no longer serving as city marshal, because he would not have tolerated such behavior.

229

FOOTNOTES

1. There are some interesting biographical comments on Allie in Boyer's *True West* article of March/April, 1976, and in Holladay, "Earp Clan." There are many scattered references to her in the Earp file, Colton Public Library.

2. Allie's death was reported in the Western press. For example, the *Phoenix Gazette* of November 15, 1947, headlined an article, "Mrs. Virgil Earp Dies at 98; Last of Famous Family." Carl Chafin has provided me with three fascinating letters from Hildreth Halliwell to Western writers in which Hildreth's relationship with the Earp family is spelled out, and in which she lambasts Frank Waters for deceiving Allie.

3. Halliwell to Mr. Sullivan, Feb. 1967.

4. Waters never changed his mind. In 1987 he repeated these uneven anti-Earp assertions: Frank Waters, "Roots and Literary Influences," in Judy Nolte Lensink (ed.), *Old Southwest, New Southwest* (Tucson, 1987), pp. 7-15.

5. Elliott West, "The Saloon in Territorial Arizona," *Journal of the West*, XIII (July 1974), 61-73.

6. Gary L. Cunningham, "Chance, Culture and Compulsion: The Gambling Games of the Kansas Cattle Towns," *Nevada Historical Society Quarterly*, XXVI (Winter, 1983), 255-71.

7. Halliwell to Sullivan, Feb. 21, 1967; "No she did not hate Wyatt although she did not like him too well as he was a bit of a show off and took all of the credit for things that Uncle Virge really did."

8. Chafin (ed.), Parsons diary, p. 155.

9. Ibid., p. 156.

APPENDIX 1
LAW AND ORDER

From 1862, when he joined the Union Army, until his death in 1905 while serving as a deputy sheriff, Virgil Walter Earp held or sought numerous law enforcement positions. In some cases he won elections; in other cases he received appointments to positions. On a few occasions he sought office but was denied an appointment, or was defeated at the polls.

The following list chronicles Virgil Earp's association with law and order, with party politics, and also with other events or occupations that can be interpreted as belonging to those either in authority, or those representing authority. Throughout his adult life, Virgil Earp was a full member of the establishment.

1862-1865	Private, 83rd Illinois Vol. Inft. Regiment
1877	U. S. mails, delivery contract, Prescott
1877	Deputy sheriff, Yavapai County [unpaid; appointed by Sheriff Ed Bowers]
1878, Sept. 3	Nightwatchman, appointed, Village of Prescott
1878, Nov.	Constable, elected, Prescott Precinct
1878, Dec.	Resigned as nightwatchman; retained constable position

1879, Nov. 27	Deputy U. S. marshal, appointed in Prescott by U. S. marshal of Arizona Territory, C. P. Dake
1879-81	Member, Hose Co. #1, Tombstone Fire Department
1880, Oct. 28	Assistant village marshal, appointed, Tombstone
1880, Nov. 12	Lost election, village marshal, Tombstone
1880, Nov. 15	Resigned, assistant village marshal, Tombstone
1881, Jan.	Lost election, city chief of police, Tombstone
1881, June 6	Acting chief of police, appointed, Tombstone [chief of police was the official title; the residents and the press usually referred to him as city marshal]
June 18	Chief of police, appointed, Tombstone
Oct. 29	Suspended as chief of police [after shootout]
1884, Aug.	Delegate, elected, Republican Party County Convention, San Bernardino
1886, June	Earp Detective Bureau, Colton
1886, July 2	Constable, elected, Village of Colton
1887, July 11	City marshal, elected, newly created City of Colton
1888, April	City marshal, re-elected, Colton
1889, March 9	Resigned as city marshal, Colton
1889, June	Member, coroner's jury, Colton
1894, Nov. 6	Constable candidate, defeated, Vanderbilt, Needles Township, San Bernardino County

1898, Nov.	Special court constable, appointed, Prescott
1900, Sept.	Sheriff candidate, Yavapai County [withdrew]
1905, Jan. 26	Deputy sheriff, appointed, Esmeralda County, Nevada; died, October 19, 1905, while deputy sheriff.

The above list does not include stints as a law officer in Wichita and Dodge City; Virgil claimed such service, but there is no substantiation for it as yet. On the other hand, there are other positions of "authority" which could be listed, such as the many fights that he refereed, and his long service as a stage driver, where he was entrusted with the care of passengers, the U. S. mails, and many a rich Wells, Fargo treasure box.

APPENDIX 2

There is no massive collection of Virgil Earp Papers, and although he was mentioned frequently in the newspapers of the day, there are not many detailed accounts that can be attributed to him. However, the following, from the San Francisco *Daily Examiner* of May 27, 1882, merits attention because it encapsulates much of his thinking, and in most things fits with what is known of his career to that time. There are a few oddities—such as mentioning Wyatt's preference for the Democratic rather than Republican party—but overall the following account can be considered vintage Virgil.

* * * * *

VIRGIL W. EARP
He Comes to San Francisco for Surgical Treatment
Shot and Crippled for Life
Admission that the Earp Party Killed Stillwell
Statement That They will Surrender.

At Port Costa Thursday noon, on the Southern Pacific Express train, an EXAMINER representative met Virgil Earp of Tombstone, Arizona. The Earp boys have figured conspicuously in print for several months past in connection with numerous murderous affrays with the cowboys about Tombstone and Tucson, involving loss of life on both sides, including the assassination of Morgan Earp by Frank Stilwell while the former was playing billiards in a Tombstone saloon, and the subsequent killing of Stillwell by the Earp party. For the killing of Stillwell the Earps were pursued by the Sheriff of Cochise county, and are still in refuge. Reports have widely differed in placing the responsibility for the crimes committed, as well as establishing the cause of the trouble, the friends on each side warmly reciprocating in picturing the other side in the worst lights of ruffianism. Virgil Earp is not a ruffian in appearance. He was found in a sleeping car, smoking a cigar. His face, voice and manner were prepossessing. He is close to six feet in height, of medium build, chestnut hair, sandy mustache, light eyebrows, quiet, blue eyes and frank expression., He wore a wide-brimmed, slate-colored slouch hat, pants of a brown and white stripes, and a blue diagonal coat and vest, both the latter with bullet holes in them, bearing testimony of a recent fight when he was shot in the back, the bullet coming out at the front of his vest,. His left arm was carried in a sling, also a memento of his last fight, when he received a bullet in his arm, since causing the loss of about six inches of bone and which cripples him for life. The wounded arm is the cause of his visit to this city, where he seeks surgical aid in hope of so far recovering its use that he may be able to dress himself unassisted.

The injured member kept him in severe pain, increased by the jarring of the cars, in which he had come from Colton, where he had been on a visit to his parents and to bury his brother Morgan. Questioned concerning his experience in Arizona, together with other details of his life, he answered pleasantly and told his story as follows:

STORY OF HIS LIFE

I was born in Kentucky, but was raised in Illinois and Iowa. My parents came to the State, settling in San Bernardino, near Colton, at which latter place they now live. I served for a little over three years in the war, in an Illinois regiment, and came to California in 1866. I soon went into New Mexico, Arizona, and all that Southern country, where I have spent nearly six years. When Tombstone was discovered I was in Prescott. The first stage that went out of Prescott toward Tombstone was robbed. Robberies were frequent and became expensive, and the disordered condition of the new country soon brought a demand for the better protection of business and money, as well as life. I was asked to go to Tombstone in my capacity as United States Marshal, and went. My brother Wyatt and myself were fairly well treated for a time, but when the desperate characters who were congregated there, and who had been unaccustomed to troublesome molestation by the authorities, learned that we meant business and were determined to stop their rascality if possible, they began to make it warm for us. The Tombstone country is of a peculiar character, the community being unsettled and dangerous. Most of the business men there stay simply to make money enough to live somewhere else comfortably, and, of course, the greatest object with them is to have as much money as possible spent in the town and to get as much of it as they can, careless of the means of dispensation or the results of rough manners. Aside from the legitimate business men the bulk of the residents are idle or desperate characters, most of them coming into town broke and depending upon the gambling table or criminal ventures to supply them with means of livelihood and dissipation.

THE COWBOYS

At one time numbered about 200, but during the last two years about fifty of them have been killed. The most of them are what we call "saddlers," living almost wholly in the saddle, and largely engaged in raiding into Sonora, and adjacent country and stealing cattle, which they sell in Tombstone. It is rarely that any of these stolen cattle are recovered. When the thieves are closely pursued, and it seems likely that they will be overhauled and the stock recovered, the cowboys sell the cattle to some of the butchers practically in partnership with them, and I know of cases where the finest cattle in the country have been sold at a dollar a head. When cattle are not handy the cowboys rob stages and engage in similar enterprises to raise money. As soon as they are in funds they ride into town, drink, gamble and fight. They spend their money as free as water in the saloons, dancehouses or faro banks, and this is one reason they have so many friends in town. All that large class of degraded characters who gather the crumbs of such carouses stand ready to assist them out of any trouble or into any paying rascality. The saloons and gambling houses, into whose treasuries most of the money is ultimately turned, receive them cordially and must be called warm friends of the cowboys. A good many of the merchants fear to express themselves against the criminal element, because they want to keep the patronage of the cowboys' friends, and the result is that when any conflict between officers and cattle thieves or stage robbers occurs, followed up by shootings around town, as witnessed during the last few months, most of the expression of opinion comes from the desperado class and their friends, and the men who should speak loudest and most decisively to correct the condition of affairs are generally the quietest. An officer doing his duty must rely almost entirely upon his own conscience for encouragement. The sympathy of the respectable portion of the community may be with him, but it is not openly expressed.

THE BAD ELEMENT

Knows its advantage in this respect, and makes the most of it. The cowboys are collected from all parts of the Western country, from which they have been crowded by advancing civilization, and they know that Arizona is about the only place left for them to operate in as an organization. With a complete breaking up of the company threatened in event of losing their hold where they are now, they resist official interference with the greatest desperation. Concerning the fights between the cowboys and myself and brothers, it has been stated over and over again that there was an old feud between us and some of our enemies, and that we were fighting only to revenge personal wrongs and gratify personal hatred. All such statements are false. We went into Tombstone to do our duty as officers. To do that we were put in conflict with a band of desperadoes, and it resolved itself into a question of which side could first drive the other out of the country, or kill them in it. To-day my brother Morg is dead, and I am a cripple for life. My other brothers are fugitives, but they will give themselves up. It was our boys who killed Stilwell.

BEFORE STILWELL DIED

He confessed that he killed Morg, and gave the names of those who were implicated with him. When my brothers were leaving Arizona, they got dispatches from Tucson saying that Stilwell and a party of friends were watching all the railroad trains passing that way, and were going through them in search of all Earps and their friends, carrying short shotguns under their overcoats and promising to kill on sight. Our boys were bound to look out for themselves, and when they got near Tucson were very cautious. They found Stilwell near the track and killed him. For the first time the Sheriff has shown anxiety to arrest some one, and the boys are keeping out of his way. The Court in Tombstone does not sit again for six months yet, and they don't want to lie in jail all that time waiting for trial, but when the Court sits again they will give themselves up, and with fair play, will be acquitted. The press dispatches that have been sent here have been very unfair to us and have been made to conform to a plan to carry all these fights into politics this season. I am a Republican. My brothers are Democrats. I am sorry to see that thing taken into politics as a personal measure, because the true aspect of the trouble will be lost and new enmities are likely to be created. I heard that Doc Holliday, one of our friends about whom there has been considerable talk, had been captured at Denver. Word was sent me that he would be taken out on a writ of habeas corpus, and that before an officer from the Territory could reach him he would be released. I do not know if he succeeded in getting off or not. There was

SOMETHING VERY PECULIAR

About Doc. He was gentlemanly, a good dentist, a friendly man, and yet outside of us boys I don't think he had a friend in the Territory. Tales were told that he had murdered men in different parts of the country, that he had robbed and stolen and committed all manner of crimes, and yet when persons were asked how they knew it they could only admit that it was hearsay, and that nothing of

241

the kind had been in reality traced up to Doc's account. He was a slender, sickly fellow, but whenever a stage was robbed or a row started, and help was needed, Doc was one of the first to saddle his horse and report for duty. The stories, at one time widely circulated, that we were in with the cowboys and quarreled over the division of the spoils, was ridiculous. It was at least disbelieved by Wells, Fargo & Co., who I represented, and while I was City Marshal they gave me this. The speaker here displayed on the inside of his coat a large gold badge, a five-pointed star set inside of a circular band, inscribed on one side, "City Marshal, Tombstone, A.T.," and on the other, "V. W. Earp, with Compliments of Wells, Fargo, & Co." Mr. Earp was in such pain that for the time his story was cut short. He was met at Oakland by two friends, who accompanied him to this city, where he will remain about thirty days. Yesterday he placed himself under the care of a leading surgeon and was unable to receive visitors, keeping himself well secluded. His escape from death by his last wounds was remarkable. Besides the shot which crippled his arm he was shot clean through the body, and upon the day following that upon which the dead body of his brother reached the home of his parents, he, too, arrived at Colton, expecting to die. Though in good health otherwise his arm will prevent any further active participation in the sensational warfare against the cowboys.

BIBLIOGRAPHY

MANUSCRIPTS/ARCHIVES

Berkeley, California, Bancroft Library.

Interviews, Virgil and Wyatt Earp.

Cambridge, Mass., Harvard University Library.

Houghton Collection.

Colton, California, Colton Public Library.

Earp Family Collection.

Columbia, Missouri, State Historical Society.

Barton County Records.

Laguna Niguel, Calif., Federal Records Center/National

Archives. Legal Records, Third Judicial District, Territory

of Arizona.

Los Angeles, Seaver Center for Western History Research,

Natural History Museum.

William S. Hart Papers [Wyatt Earp correspondence].

McLean, Virginia, U. S. Marshal's Office.

Arizona Marshal's Office Correspondence.

Monmouth, Illinois, Wyatt Earp Birthplace Museum.

Earp Family Papers.

New York City, New-York Historical Society.

Will McLaury Papers.

Pella, Iowa, Central College Library.

Earp Family Papers.

Phoenix, State Archives.

Yavapai County, criminal and civil cases; Justice Court records; Third Judicial District Papers.

Prescott, Sharlot Hall Museum.

Clipping file; pamphlet file; Yavapai County records; photographs; city directories; Great Registers.

Reno, Nevada Historical Society.

Misc. Papers of Virgil and Wyatt Earp.

San Bernardino, San Bernardino Public Library.

Local history papers and clippings.

San Francisco, Wells, Fargo Bank.

Earp Bros. Papers.

San Marino, California, Huntington Library.

Stuart N. Lake Papers; Fred Dodge Papers.

Springfield, Illinois, State Historical Society.

Adjutant General's Papers [Civil War].

Tombstone, Carl Chafin Collection.

Typescripts, with indices, of George W. Parsons Diaries; biographical files; Tombstone historical summaries.

Tucson, Arizona Historical Society.

Lincoln Ellsworth Papers; biographical files; minutes, Tombstone Common Council; Medigovitch Collection [Tombstone files]; George Whitwell Parsons Diaries.

Tucson, Pima County, Recorder's Office.

Wyatt Earp commission, resignation; mining claims.

Tucson, University of Arizona, Special Collections.

John Clum papers; Wyatt Earp Papers; Walter Noble Burns Collection. Washington, D.C., National Archives. Old Army Records; Pension Files [Mexican War; Civil War].

BOOKS

Ball, Larry D. *The United States Marshals of New Mexico and Arizona Territories, 1846-1912*. Albuquerque, 1978.

Boyer, Glenn. *I Married Wyatt Earp: The Recollections of Josephine Sarah Marcus Earp*. Tucson, 1976.

Boyer, Glenn. *The Suppressed Murder of Wyatt Earp*. San Antonio, 1976.

Breakenridge, William M. *Helldorado: Bringing the Law to the Mesquite*. Boston, 1928.

Dodge, Fred. *Undercover For Wells Fargo*. Boston, 1969.

Galbraith, F. W. *Minerals of Arizona*. Bulletin 149, Arizona Bureau of Mines, Tucson, 1941.

Harlow, W. S. *Duties of Sheriffs and Constables*. San Francisco, 1884.

Kelly, Geo. H. (comp.) *Legislative History: Arizona, 1864-1912*. Tucson, 1926.

Kintop, Jeffrey M., and Rocha, Guy Louis. *The Earps' Last Frontier: Wyatt and Virgil Earp in the Nevada Mining Camps, 1902-1905*. Reno, 1990.

Lake, Stuart N. *Wyatt Earp: Frontier Marshal*. New York, 1931.

Martin, Douglas. *Tombstone's Epitaph*. Albuquerque, 1958.

Place's Southern California Guide. Los Angeles, 1886.

Prassel, Frank Richard. *The Western Peace Officer: A Legacy of Law and Order*. Norman, Okla., 1972.

The Private Journal of George Whitwell Parsons. Phoenix, 1939.

Quebbeman, Frances E. *Medicine in Territorial Arizona*. Phoenix, 1966.

Shillinberg, William B. *Wyatt Earp & the "Buntline Special" Myth*. Tucson, 1976.

Turner, Alford E. *The Earps Talk*. College Station, Texas, 1980.

Turner, Alford E. *The O. K. Corral Inquest*. College Station, Texas, 1981.

Wagoner, Jay W. *Arizona Territory, 1863-1912: A Political History*.Tucson, 1970.

Waters, Frank. *The Earp Brothers of Tombstone: The Story of Mrs. Virgil Earp*. New York, 1960.

ARTICLES

Arizona Quarterly Illustrated, 1880-81.

Ball, Larry D. "Pioneer Lawman: Crawley P. Dake and Law Enforcement on the Southwestern Frontier," *Journal of Arizona History*, XIV (Autumn, 1973), 243-56.

Bishop, Wm. Henry. "Across Arizona," *Harper's New Monthly Magazine*, LXVI (March, 1883), 493-502.

Blake, Wm. P. "Geology and Veins of Tombstone," *Transactions, American Institute of Mining Engineers*, X (1882), 334-49.

Blandy, John F. "The Mining Region Around Prescott, Arizona," *Transactions, American Institute of Mining Engineers*, XI (1883), 286-91.

Boyer, Glenn. "Johnny Behan of Tombstone," *Frontier Times*, July, 1976, pp. 6-9, 55-57.

Boyer, Glenn. "Those Marryin' Earp Men," *True West*, March/April, 1976, pp. 14-21, 17.

Clum, John P. "It All Happened in Tombstone," *Arizona Historical Review*, II (October, 1929), 46-72.

Cunningham, Gary L. "Chance, Culture and Compulsion: The Gambling Games of the Kansas Cattle Towns," *Nevada Historical Society Quarterly*, XXVI (Winter, 1983), 255-71.

Fireman, Bert. "Fremont's Arizona Adventure," *American West*, I (Winter, 1964), 9-19.

Holladay, Fred. "The Earp Brothers in Goldfield," in *Nevada Official Bicentennial Book*. Las Vegas, 1976.

Holladay, Fred. "As Rich as Vanderbilt," *Heritage Tales* [San Bernardino Historical Society], II (1979), 1-16.

Holladay, Fred. "The Earp Clan in San Bernardino County," *Heritage Tales* [San Bernardino Historical Society], I (1978), 101-117.

Holladay, Fred. "Judge Earp," *Odyssey* [San Bernardino Historical Society], II (January, 1980), 1-3.

Murbarger, Nell. "The Deserted New Yorks," *True West*, January/February, 1965, pp. 12-15, 68-69.

"Prescott, Arizona," *Mining & Scientific Press*, August 9, 1877, p. 81.

"Prescott and Vicinity," *Mining & Scientific Press*, November 17, 1877, p. 306.

"Report of Mission Agency, August 20, 1888," in *Report of the Secretary of the Interior*. Washington, 1888, II, 10-20.

"Rousseau Diary: Across the Desert to California, from Salt Lake to San Bernardino in 1864," *Quarterly, San Bernardino County Museum Association*, VI (Winter, 1958), 1-17.

Searles, Lin. "The Short Unhappy Life of Johnny-Behind-The-Deuce," *Frontier Times*, December-January, 1966, pp. 22-23, 44.

Spude, Robert L. "A Land of Sunshine and Silver: Silver Mining in Central Arizona, 1871-1885," *Journal of Arizona History*, XVI (Spring, 1975), 29-76.

Underhill, Lonnie E. "The Tombstone Discovery: Recollections of Ed Schieffelin & Richard Gird," *Arizona and the West*, XXI (Spring, 1979), 37-75.

Walker, Henry P. "Arizona Land Fraud: Model 1880; The Tombstone Townsite Company," *Arizona and the West*, XXI (Spring, 1979), 5-36.

Waters, Frank. "Roots and Literary Influences," in Judy Nolte Lensink (ed.), *Old Southwest, New Southwest* (Tucson, 1987), pp. 7-15.

247

West, Elliott. "The Saloon in Territorial Arizona," *Journal of the West*, XIII (July, 1974), 61-73.
"Yavapai County Mines," *Engineering & Mining Journal*, February 27, June 19, 1897.

NEWSPAPERS

Colton *Courier*
Colton *Semi-Tropic*
Dodge City *Globe*
Goldfield News
Goldfield Review
Lamar Republican (Missouri)
Los Angeles *Daily Star*
Los Angeles *Evening Express*
Los Angeles *Herald*
Los Angeles *Morning Journal*
Los Angeles *News*
Los Angeles *Times*
Phoenix *Arizona Republican*
Phoenix *Gazette*
Phoenix Herald
Pioche Record (Nevada)
Portland *Oregonian*
Prescott *Arizona Weekly Journal-Miner*
Prescott *Arizona Enterprise*
Redlands *Citrograph*
Riverside *Morning Enterprise*
San Bernardino *Daily/Weekly Courier*
San Bernardino *Daily/Weekly Times*
San Bernardino *Kaleidoscope*
San Diego *Union*
Tombstone Epitaph

Tombstone Nugget
Tombstone Prospector
Tucson *Arizona Daily/Weekly Citizen*
Tucson *Arizona Daily Star*
Wilmington Journal (California)

OTHER

Chafin, Carl (ed.) "The West of George Whitwell Parsons," typescripts of several of the annual diaries of Parsons; I have used those of 1880-1883. These have been carefully edited and bound in individual volumes for each year; copies have been deposited in the Library, Arizona Historical Society, Tucson.

Halliwell, Hildreth. Interview of 1971 with Alford Turner and A. Oster, tapes in Media Services, University of Arizona Library, Tucson.

Jones, Clark Harding. "A History of the Development and Progress of Colton, California, 1873-1900," M. A. Thesis, Claremont Graduate School, 1951, copy in Colton Public Library.

INDEX

251